Inside Out

Inside Out

Edith Young

Routledge & Kegan Paul   London

First published 1971
by Routledge and Kegan Paul Ltd
Broadway House,
68–74 Carter Lane,
London, EC4V 5EL
Printed in Great Britain
at the St Ann's Press,
Park Road, Altrincham
Set in 11/12 pt. Linotype Plantin
© Edith Young 1971

I S B N 0 7100 6997 9

Contents

List of Illustrations

1   Dublin

The house in Drumcondra, Dublin, where I was born appears to me now as if it had been bombed. The front door is there: and so is the grey Irish sky through the fanlight. A glossy wallpaper, the colour of treacle, embossed with a pattern like that on the linings of musty cupboards in deserted houses, is intact in the long narrow hall. So dark is it that I can scarcely see the faded carpet on the staircase leading to a door on the first landing which I know is that of the 'return room'. Everything in the room is familiar enough, especially a mirror hanging by a window filled with the summer green of trees at the end of the garden. Reflected in the mirror is a little girl in a clumsy woollen frock, wearing black stockings and boots, a sun-bonnet perched, as though ready for flight, on a cloud of flaxen hair. Eyes stare back at me. The door behind me opens, and my cousin, Irene, peers in.

'Is it admiring yourself in the glass you are? On a fine warm morning like this. You should be out in the garden.'

As though breasting water she glides across the dunduckety-mud-coloured carpet to tower over me in the glass. Her golden hair is wound round her head like a coronet. Eyes as amber as her necklace are bent on mine. She is all I long to be. I shrink from her, as she removes my sun-bonnet, strokes back my hair and exposes the broad width of forehead I believe to be unbecoming in a girl.

'Irene,' I say, arresting her hand, 'I'm a plain child, amn't I?'

'Vain, I'm afraid,' she reproaches. A tender smile gives me courage to repeat the question.

'Who on earth put that idea into your head?'

'Mother. I heard her say to Granny the other day that if I wasn't exactly ugly, she would have to admit that I am plain.'

She ponders on this in silence, and then says we shouldn't believe all we hear.

'But if it's true,' I complain, 'nobody will want to marry me when I grow up. I want to be beautiful like you.'

'Beauty,' she reflects slowly and with a gravity that has left a lasting impression, 'is in the eye of the beholder.'

On her hands and knees polishing the hall floor, Mary-Ann, the servant girl, pauses in her work when she hears the chapel bell tolling for a funeral in Glasnevin Cemetery. To muffle its sound I clasp hands to my ears.

'Another poor soul gone to Kingdom Come. May he rest in peace,' says Mary-Ann, piously crossing herself.

A perpetually smiling angel, guarding with glistening wings a fine marble tomb at the entrance to the cemetery, thrust a rounded arm and shapely hand to point a finger to a rent of blue in a passing cloud to tell me I should look for Kingdom Come in the sky.

To be dead was to be like a stoat, cold, stiff, and helpless, lying on the path hedged by box. I had stooped to examine its delicate pink claws before my grandfather tossed it on the ferrule of his stick, as he might a piece of waste paper, to a grassy grave.

'Dead as a door nail,' he remarked in excuse. 'Dead as that poor devil beyond there in the hearse.'

With a flourish of his blackthorn he heralded the arrival of a funeral cortège at the cemetery gates. Sleek black horses, apparelled like princes, the nodding black plumes on their heads keeping time to the pace of their hooves on the frosty ground, were driven by poker-faced mutes, their top hats garlanded by bands of crêpe. We had to step aside to allow them to pass. As the hearse — a show-case of autumnal flowers — came alongside the chapel door and the funeral flunkeys jumped down from the box seat to fling open the doors of the carriages for the mourners to alight, my grandfather nudged me.

'All the king's horses and all the king's men,' he said with a chuckle, 'couldn't put Humpty Dumpty together again. The money that's wasted on a turn-out like that would keep many a poor soul alive for more than a twelvemonth; granny, yourself, and me into the bargain.'

Granny bid Mary-Ann take me with her for a treat to the Liffey. On landing from a horse tram on the quays, she had her work cut out to get me to budge from the doorstep of a miser's decaying house, where, on a visit with my grandfather, I had lost the brand new penny he had shyly thrust in my hand at parting. Grandpa said I should treasure it as a keepsake from an old skinflint who had never before been known to part with a brass farthing in all his life. I wanted to see if I could wheedle another out of him, but Mary-Ann wouldn't hear of it. Misers, in her opinion, were no whit better than thieves. And if I didn't 'come along of her without more ado' she'd hand me over to one of them there 'policemen' keeping watch by the bales of goods on the wharf.

Not until she had promised me a stick of my favourite sugar stick, known as Peggy's Leg, could I be persuaded to leave the noise and bustle of the quay to follow her to a street of slum tenements in the vicinity.

A dirty drab street. Ragged children playing hopscotch on a slimy pavement. Heads were thrust from windows to watch us pass by. Potato peelings lay scattered on doorsteps. Blousy women paused in their gossiping to bid Mary-Ann a 'good day'.

In response to a resounding knock on a door, scabbed by peeling paint, of a once fine Georgian house, a bleary, red-faced woman scowled at us from under the hood of a black shawl.

'What call had ye to bring the girlie to a house of mourning?' she scolded. 'It's no place at all for the likes of her.'

'The ould lady was that set on my taking her that I daren't refuse. I wouldn't have brought her if I could have helped it,' whined Mary-Ann.

She thrust me into a sour smelling hall, banged the door to, and was for leaving me to her mother, who promised to find me a sweetie, if I'd come along of her, while Mary-Ann paid respects to her Da. I wriggled from her grasp, wailed to be taken home, and clinging to the skirt of her daughter, ran at her heels up a flight of bare wooden stairs. She paused at the landing to warn me that if she heard a word out of me she'd call her Ma. Cautiously, and with as much hesitation as though she were about to enter a cell of the condemned, she turned the handle and pushed open the door of a room that seemed to be blanketed in a yellow fog. Hardly a chink of daylight showed through a window covered by a blind. Three candles alight in a saucer standing on the marble slab of a washstand showed up what looked like a white mound on a bed in the far corner of the room. I tiptoed in after her and she closed the door.

Laying a finger to her lips she approached the bed. Crossing herself she slumped on her knees by the bedside to pray.

'Mother of Consolation, Tower of Ivory, Star of the Sea, Holy Mother of God, have mercy on his soul,' she muttered. The lovely names of the Virgin seemed to weave a spell.

I discovered that a sheet drawn taut across the bed covered all but the head and hands of what appeared to be an old man. So sound asleep was he that not even her prayers could disturb him. Now I knew why she had cautioned me to silence. The flickering candle-light showed up a nose that stuck out like a beak over shrunken lips. A quiff of dark hair, like a duck's wing, was plastered to a forehead as waxen as the hands which lay crossed on his chest like those of an effigy on a tomb.

Prompted by an impulse I could not resist, I stretched out a hand to lay it on his. The unresponsive coldness was like an electric shock. I snatched my hand away as from a live coal; and letting out a piercing scream, threw myself, sobbing as though my heart would break, on the frayed pattern of roses on the linoleum at the foot of the bed.

Mary-Ann had taken me in her arms and was trying to soothe me, wiping my tear-stained cheeks with her work-hardened hand, when her mother, alarmed I suppose by my scream, came scuttling into the room.

'What in the name of God have you been doing to the child?' she scolded. 'She's making enough noise to wake the dead.'

'I never laid hands on her,' said Mary-Ann ruefully. 'What ails you, my pet?' she asked, anxiously searching the face I had hidden in her shawl for a bump or a bruise that might explain my distress.

'The sooner you take her out of this the better,' advised her mother. 'It's my belief she's seen a ghost.'

Once clear of the house my sobs subsided. 'Promise me like a good girl,' entreated Mary-Ann, 'that you'll not let on to your Granny where you've been this day. If she knew you'd seen my poor Da laid out for burial, you'd soon see the last of me.' Her eyes filled with tears. She'd remember me in her prayers to her dying day, if I promised not to get her into trouble . . .

From that day to this, I never willingly enter a room in which either a blind or a curtain has been drawn over a window in daylight; nor do I pull the curtains at night. I have feared death ever since.

For evidence of my parents' presence in my birthplace I have to rely on a photograph, faded by being many years stored away in a family album, showing them seated on a couch in the 'return room'. The curiosity which many a time has driven me to study that '*fadagraph*' has imprinted it on my mind.

My mother wears her hair piled on top of her head in the Edwardian style. A fringe, softening her width of brow, shortens the length of her oval face. The sweet and deprecating smile she turns to my father belies the queenliness of one who bore the name of Eleanor. My father's delicate — and, I always considered — beautiful hand rests on the leg-of-mutton sleeve which encases her arm.

Father's profile, his sensuous lips curved in a smile, regards her through pince-nez attached to a broad ribbon. With hair brushed back from his forehead to the nape of his neck, a width of tie knotted with a studied negligence under a white collar worn over what would appear to be a black velvet jacket, he could have been posing for a portrait of a romantic poet of the nineties. There they were before I can remember them.

I think of my mother in her youth as a firebird, moulting in the confines of her home, who was set free by the attractive young Scotsman, who had come knocking on the door in search of the board and lodging he had seen advertised in the *Irish Times*.

When he turned up out of the blue, she was the only member of the family living at home. Her elder sister — Irene's mother — who, it is said, had dominated the household had been for some years married to a Presbyterian clergyman. He was done to death, so the story goes, by an explosion from a magic lantern whilst showing slides of the Holy Land to children at the Sunday School. Her younger sister had gone to St Patrick Dunn's hospital to be trained as a nurse; and her brother, an eccentric with literary leanings, but talent only for making money, was busy accumulating a small fortune from the tailoring establishments he had scattered throughout Dublin.

My grandmother had not at first approved of the ideas my father had absorbed at the weekly meetings he attended at the Theosophical Headquarters at Ely Place. But since he always had a soft word for her and an engaging twinkle in his eye he succeeded in gaining her permission to allow my mother to accompany him to listen to the words let fall from the lips of that female sage, Madam Blavatsky.

My mother insisted on attributing what she was pleased to call my 'happy disposition' to the fact that I was a child of love. I concluded that she meant one of two things: either that I was the first fruit of my parents' youthful ardour, or that I was conceived out of wedlock. I suspect that if a growing mutual interest in theosophy united her to my father in spirit, too close a proximity to him in the home of her parents united her to him in the flesh before the union was sanctioned by marriage.

My father was not earning much as a clerk in an insurance company, not enough anyway to provide my mother with a home of her own. They had to rent the top storey of my grandparents' house. It must have been humiliating to my mother to have to share her parents' house, especially with two young children. If, as I believe, she left me almost exclusively to the care of my grandmother after the birth of my brother, I naturally felt rejected.

My father always spoke of his youth in Dublin as of a paradise lost. On returning from attending a theosophical meeting on a Sunday evening, relaxing in an easy chair by the fireside in our later London suburban home, he could be beguiled into entertaining his family by recalling his youth.

His description of George Russell — better known by his pseudonym, A.E., poet and publicist, editor of the *Irish Homestead*, whom Joyce as Stephen Daedalus encounters in several scenes in *Ulysses*—re-introduced me to a bearded, bespectacled Irish god of the sea on whose 'homespun' knee I had been nursed as a child. He expressed his appreciation of a lasting friendship by dedicating his collected poems to father.

A.E. in his time played many parts. As an orator he rose to address a theosophical gathering in Ely Place on the legacy ancient Ireland had bequeathed to her poets. According to father, he spoke of her legendary heroes, *Cuhulan, Finn McCool, Deirdre of the Sorrows, Fergus of the Brazen Car*, as though they had been his intimates. As a believer in Blavatsky's occult lore, he imagined that his short-sighted eyes saw what others failed to see: fairies, the banshee, sylphs and undines disporting themselves in some lonely glen at twilight, 'when the mists do be gathering over the hills and there's not a sound to be heard but the cry of a curlew'. He was to be seen cycling along the Cabinteely road on a Saturday afternoon, canvas and painting gear strapped to his back, on his way to meet the old gods of Ireland in the Wicklow hills. There were several of his paintings in each home of ours in my youth. In one shawled peasant girls peered through the mists at the mount of Ben Bulben.

If pressed by me, father would admit that as a poet A.E. had neither the stature nor talent of Yeats; but that humanly, and as a man who practised his ideals, he was supreme.

Father, who usually referred to Yeats as Willy, gave an account of Willy trying his hand at magic. In a fine old Georgian house a staircase took him to a bare back room in which he was to join the privileged few chosen by Yeats to witness the rite. An opulent marble mantelpiece stood in the stead of an altarpiece. Wine bottles acted as sconces for the candles by whose light Yeats was to chalk a pentagram on the floorboards. The stage thus set, the audience squatted cross-legged against the wall. Into their midst strode Yeats, garbed in black, like the priest of some forgotten cult, a raven lock sweeping his brow, to chant a mantrum designed to call into being apparitions from the nether world. Into his hand a participant placed a slaughtered cock; and in accordance with the instructions of those versed in the black arts, Yeats, holding the sacrificial bird at arm's length, whilst droning an incantation, sprinkled blood from its matted feathers into the middle of the mystical five pointed star.

'What happened? Did you see anything?' I eagerly enquired.

'All I saw,' father confessed, 'was Willy turning away in disgust from the dead bird at his feet. But if nothing came of his tricks, it was well worth my while to have been there. To hear him expound the mysteries of the Caballa or recite one of his early lyrics over a bottle of wine afterwards was an experience I'm not likely to forget. Tone deaf though he was reported to be, I have yet to meet the man who had as fine an ear for the music of words as had Willy. He was too intellectual ever to have become a medium.'

No one he knew could beat Madam Blavatsky in that respect. The old lady was a master in the art.

'Maybe she fooled me,' he reflected, stroking his chin. 'But I swear I saw her conjure flowers from the vacant air. In obedience to an imperious wave of her hand, pansies, violets, an odd rose or two, would come fluttering down from the chandelier into her capacious lap.'

If mother suggested that Blavatsky had hypnotized him, or I that she had the flowers concealed either in the chandelier or up her sleeve, he would shake his head and reprove her with a bantering: 'Oh ye of little faith! Seeing is believing. I swear I saw the flowers she had materialized.'

He had handled them and had even received a posy of violets from the old lady which he had proudly stuck in his buttonhole to prove to mother that what he claimed for Blavatsky was true. But, alas, he had either lost her token of regard on the way home or it had mysteriously vanished in some other way.

He did not believe that Blavatsky set much store by those tricks. She merely performed them to amuse her devotees. An inveterate smoker, he had seen her stretch out her hand to a box of her special brand of Russian cigarettes in a distant corner of the room and without further to-do a cigarette was between her fingers.

Impressed as he was, he thought those performances a mistake on her part. It gave evidence to those who were only too ready to condemn her as a charlatan without having read a line of either *Isis Unveiled* or her monumental work, *The Secret Doctrine*.

'Extraordinary woman — Blavatsky,' he would conclude with an amused and pensive smile. 'I count it a privilege to have known her.'

Although my father could only claim to have had a nodding acquaintance with Joyce, Joyce paid him the dubious compliment of derisively coupling his name in *Ulysses* with that of W. Q. Judge (an American theosophist promoted by Blavatsky to act as General Secretary of the Society) and A.E.

Yogi, bogey, box: Dunlop, Judge, A.E., he scoffs. Father in his turn gave a none too flattering description of Joyce as a non-descript, shabby-genteel young fellow, thin-lipped and taciturn, who would as well bark at you as give you a civil answer to a question you were bold enough to put to him.

He had many a time seen him sitting by himself at a table in a far corner of a vegetarian restaurant they had mutually fre-quented. Picking at a nut cutlet, he kept his head buried in a newspaper lest anyone should have the temerity to address him.

Should father venture to hail him, he'd be met with a curt nod. No doubt he considered him and all those who attended the meet-ings at Ely Place to be deserving of ridicule.

According to father, the slim volume of verse Joyce had to his credit in those days couldn't hold a candle to that of A.E. Yet A.E. had gone out of his way to shower praise on *Pomes Penyeach . . .*

1 The author before she can remember herself being photographed, at her birthplace, 72 Drumcondra Road, Dublin

2 The author and her brother Ronald prior to departure for America (see p. 10)

3 The author's Quaker grandmother, photographed in Ireland at The Peak, Killiney (see p. 28)

When in the late thirties I drew my father's attention to Joyce's reference to him in *Ulysses,* he looked surprised.

'Well,' he said suavely, 'I'm in good company anyway.'

'A shy, proud man — was Joyce. He used his native wit as a weapon to defend himself against the literary set in Dublin who regarded him as an outsider. Once a Jesuit always a Jesuit. His attitude to religion was that of an apostate priest.'

If to have hobnobbed with the Dublin literary élite had afforded my father some compensation for the boredom of earning a living at a thankless job, it was his devotion to theosophy which offered him escape from the humiliation of sharing a home.

At the invitation of W. Q. Judge, Katherine Tingley, the President of the New York branch of the Theosophical Society, came to speak to the Dublin section of the Society. She took such a fancy to my father whom she regarded as one of Blavatsky's bright boys and the right hand of W. Q. Judge that she there and then invited him to act as her private secretary; and even went so far as to offer to pay the passage of his wife and family to the States.

Though I gathered that my mother would have preferred to go on facing the ills she knew, my father found the offer too tempting to be turned down. He may well have regarded it as an order from those mysterious beings known to theosophists as the Masters of Wisdom who were alleged by H. P. Blavatsky to have inspired her *Secret Doctrine* and to rule over the spiritual destiny of mankind from some inaccessible and remote valley of the Himalayas.

To Katherine Tingley — known to her adherents as the Purple Mother — I owe my exile from the home I knew, from grandparents who were dear to me. I landed with my parents amongst a batch of Irish immigrants on the docks at New York.

I.O.—B

2   New York

Sweltering in our winter clothes, my brother and I sat on a tin trunk. Father had gone in search of the lady who had offered us hospitality at her home in New Jersey until such time as we were able to find a home of our own in New York.

Mother held herself aloof from the other passengers in the steerage. She fidgeted with her handbag, and readjusted the toque wreathed with violets which she had purchased in a smart shop in Grafton Street to make a good impression on our hostess. Puckering her brow she paced back and forth scanning the crowd through the mesh of her veil for a sight of father.

My brother and I quarrelled. He kept blowing shrill blasts on a whistle suspended from a cord over the collar of his new sailor suit. The upturned brim of a matching sailor hat made a halo for his podgy baby face. In an attempt to get the whistle away from him, I received a kick on the shin, which I repaid by knocking him off his perch. His yell brought mother to us.

She threatened to send us packing straight back to Dublin unless we behaved ourselves. My brother whimpered.

'To Granny?' I cried jubilantly.

'Put your bonnet straight,' she ordered. 'With your hair plastered to cheeks as red as a beetroot, you look a sight.'

'What on earth can be keeping your father?' she said. 'How can I be expected to recognize Mrs Lindsay? I've never set eyes on her.'

'Has Papa?' I ventured to enquire.

'To be sure. Many an evening he spent with her and the Purple Mother at Ely Place and I waiting up past midnight for him to return.'

'Purple Mother,' I repeated, mystified. 'Who is the Purple Mother?'

'Whist!' she cautioned, fixing her eyes on a gap in the crowd. 'I've spotted him.' Her cheeks, wan from being continuously sea-sick in the sour-smelling cabin we had shared with another immigrant family, turned to a hectic red.

I climbed on the trunk. And sure enough there was my father with a lady in dazzling white, a scarlet parasol held over her head. Smiling, she offered an elegantly gloved hand to my mother.

'I guess,' said Mrs Lindsay, 'you're not sorry to be on terra firma, Mrs Dunlop. I hear you had a rough passage.'

'I had no idea,' returned mother accusingly, 'that it would be as hot as this in New York in October. The children and I are stifling in our winter clothes.'

'You've landed in a heatwave. It is seldom as warm as this in the Fall. There will be a breeze on the Hudson; and once your baggage arrives back home you can change into your summer clothes. That will be fine and dandy, won't it, kiddies?' she added, addressing us children.

Having guessed by the glance mother exchanged with father that we had no summer clothes, I averted my head. She was obliged to kiss the tip of my nose. 'Your little daughter is shy,' she remarked, smiling archly at my father.

Wedged between him and the skirt of Mrs Lindsay, I clung to the rail of the ferry which was packed tight with passengers. A track of foam followed us across the darkening Hudson. A star burnt a hole in the indigo sky above the Statue of Liberty. Mother had Ronnie in her arms. I could tell by the compression of her lips that she felt ill at ease. Was it that she felt dowdy in comparison to Mrs Lindsay? Or was she thinking of Granny? Drawing her attention to the star, I asked whether Granny could see the same stars in Dublin.

'Sure,' said my father, interrupting a conversation with Mrs Lindsay.

As the distance widened between us and the mainland, the phalanx of skyscrapers looked no more substantial than shapes cut out of cardboard. A city previously known to me as a black dot on a map became a cluster of lights against the background of a flaming sunset; the river a playground for the rainbow ribands dancing in the wake of the lamps alight on passing craft.

On the drive in a buggy through leafy woods to the Lindsays' home I kept my eyes on every turn in the twisting road. Sparkling and flickering in and out the grass by the roadside I spied what I imagined must surely be fairies. Delighted at my discovery, I tugged my father's arm.

'Papa,' I whispered loudly in his ear, 'there are fairies in America.'

'Really?' he said, feigning an interest. 'Where?'

'There. Playing hide and seek in the bushes.'

'Well!' exclaimed Mrs Lindsay, with a rippling peal of laughter, 'if that's not just too cute!'

Disconcerted, I demanded to know what was cute.

'Why, you are, Honey. It's easy to see where you come from. Only a little Irish girl could mistake glow worms for fairies.' I felt belittled in the eyes of my father. Tears of resentment against her scalded my cheeks . . .

Gone though I expect it now is, the Lindsays' fine, white, weatherboard house, with slender pillars flanking a veranda, remains in memory as a dream house, to which all tracks through autumnal woods inevitably lead. Trails of tinted virginia creeper festooned windows whose green shutters were closed against a noonday sun.

I was returning from a tour of inspection on the morning after our arrival, the pinafore mother insisted I should wear to protect my one and only decent frock filled with leaves lacquered in crimson and gold, to be confronted on the steps leading to the veranda by the son and heir. Clad in white from top to toe, his cropped red hair fitting him like a bronze casque, this princeling regarded me with the animosity of someone spoiling for a fight. The insolence of his inspection of my clothes — shabby in comparison to his — the air of authority with which he ordered me to throw away the rubbish I had collected, his podgy, freckled cheeks, or simply that he was a boy and older than myself, riled me. I took an instant dislike to Jasper Lindsay.

Measuring the distance between us, we eyed one another as though each held a revolver at the ready. He advanced towards me. I stood my ground. He gave a sharp tug to my pinafore, scattering the leaves at my feet. I flew at him in a rage, and we were engaged in a tussle in which I would doubtless have been vanquished had my father not intervened. Seizing me by the arm he delivered me from Jasper's grip and with a mild rebuke marched me indoors to breakfast.

This first quarrel proved to be a prelude to many others. His mother spoilt Jasper. He was her only child. Nothing that money could buy seemed too good for him. Nor did I hear her once tell him off for bad manners at table, or for being rude to the negro servants. He could lord it over my brother with impunity; but in me he met an equal. In revenge for refusing to allow me to play with his toys, I threw a platoon of his soldiers on a rubbish dump for which I was punished by being sent hungry to bed. He made fun of my clothes, mimicked my Irish accent; I in turn copied his nasal drawl and called his knickerbockers girl's bloomers. For this insult I was repaid by him riding full tilt at me down a track of the woods on his pony.

The petty warfare was a constant source of worry to my mother. As she dare not blame Jasper for provoking trouble, and my father was away in New York, dancing attendance on the Purple Mother, she took to punishing me. Nothing I could plead in self-defence did any good.

Russet and gold trees filled the dormer window of the bedroom I shared with my brother. I remember them waving their branches against a storm sky. My supper lay untouched on a table. Mother stood before me like a dragoon, a steely light in her eyes.

'Not another word out of you,' she shouts. 'Jasper's behaviour is no concern of mine. He's the apple of his mother's eye. He can do no wrong. I've told you repeatedly to steer clear of him. If you will insist on bringing disgrace on me by behaving like a hooligan I shall be obliged to keep you shut up here under lock and key. Maybe that'll bring you to your senses. You've been a hundred times worse since father went away.'

I detect a catch in her voice, but I harden my heart against her and stare glumly into the greying trees.

'Don't you understand,' she entreats, 'that we are dependent on his mother for every bite we eat? If the bread of charity leaves a bitter taste in the mouth beggars can't be choosers. God knows I don't stay here of my own accord.'

Her hectoring tone changes to supplication. I cannot resist it. Nor her appeal to be a good girl, for her sake, and turn a deaf ear to Jasper. Such a softened, humiliated mother needs me as her champion, and I willingly promise to do as she demands.

Much to my surprise, once I had trained myself to ignore Jasper's presence he ceased to find pleasure in tormenting me.

Goldenrod was my fleur-de-lys. Bearing a spear of it as an escutcheon I would plunge through hickory, scratch myself with brambles and land with a war whoop in a clearing where my mother sat on a log under yellowing beech, darning, while my brother deployed a troop of Jasper's cavalry on the parched grass at her feet. In the dry, clear air, silently and with the grace of skilled acrobats, leaves twirled, to be netted in my outspread pinafore. The slightest rustle, snap of a dry twig, scuttle of a squirrel, a bird call, sounded an alarm, which sent me prowling, waving my golden spear in search of a hidden foe.

The pungent scent of dead leaves is in my nostrils. The blue woodsmoke ascends in a spiral from their funeral pyre. A maple is spotlighted by sunshine. Under its flaming foliage I tread softly as if on holy ground. If I am indebted to Mrs Lindsay for nothing else, I owe to her the beauty of that tree; and a slight melancholy that hovers over the woods of New Jersey in the Fall. From her son I learnt something about the Haves of this world . . .

The flat which my father found for us in a poor and congested district of New York, the walls of its four small rooms papered in beige, seemed, in comparison with the spaciousness of the Lindsays' mansion, to be not much larger than a cardboard box. Between it and other similar blocks of flats, cluttering clear horizons, stretched a piece of wasteland, parched as a desert, covered with rubbish dumps partially concealed under a riot of nettles. Better far for mother, no doubt, to have a poor home of her own than to be obliged to share the luxurious home of another. Ragweed had replaced goldenrod, but at least there were rubbish dumps for me to mine for treasure.

The kitchen-living-room looked out on the dumps but the room apportioned to my brother and myself faced a scaffolding that towered above a new block of flats being built beside ours. I trembled lest the workmen up there should lose their balance and come tumbling down like ballast chucked from a balloon on to the piles of sand and bags of cement at the foot of the building. In bed at night I could see lights from distant buildings shining through the interstices of the scaffolding like the portholes of ships at sea; the building waited in port to take me across a vast dark ocean back to Dublin. As I imagined it pitching into cavernous waves, I grew lighthearted at the thought of being united to my grandmother.

I was afraid of heights, and suffered agonies in the elevated railway. Travelling down town from Amsterdam Avenue, I always

expected that the train would be derailed and I and everyone in
the carriage would be hurled on to the traffic below in the street.
To ward off such a catastrophe I would cling to mother with my
eyes closed. I did not mind that she scolded me for making a show
of myself in front of the other passengers, nor that she compared me unfavourably to my brave little brother who kept up a
running commentary on all that he saw from the window. I
could neither explain nor control my fear. By escaping to the
wasteland as soon as I heard such an expedition mentioned and
lying on the ground like a withered plant, I avoided being included
in a treat my brother so obviously enjoyed.

I did like clasping my hands and closing my eyes at mother's
bidding in bed at night to ask God's blessing on parents, grandparents, friends — 'for Jesus Christ's sake'. I liked thinking that
a kind Father had the well-being of our entire family in His keeping. But when she added a dose of oriental mysticism to a ritual
originally instigated by my grandmother by repeating a stanza
from Hindu scriptures dear to theosophists I trembled in fear.

Mother prepared us for the solemnity of her performance by
drawing apart and sitting as stiffly on the edge of the bed as a
prisoner in the dock. Her hypnotic stare warned me that she was
about to begin to intone:

> Never the Spirit was born,
> The Spirit shall cease to be never.
> End and beginning are dreams,
> Birthless and Deathless and changeless
> Remaineth the Spirit for ever.

Then she would pause dramatically, and I waited in dread for her
to deliver the closing line. In an ominous dying fall, like the
chapel bell at Glasnevin, she would drone:

'Dead though the house of it seems.' Shuddering, I ducked my
head beneath the bedclothes to muffle the knell.

I could not believe in the existence of the Purple Mother until
I actually was chosen amongst a group of older children from the
Theosophical Sunday School to attend a festival of youth, known
as White Lotus Day, at which she was to preside. As the gentle
mild-eyed teacher had done me the honour of picking on me to
recite an innocuous and banal poem at the great occasion, one
of father's admirers had presented me with a dainty white frock
with hair ribbon to match. Such finery changed goose-girl into

bridesmaid: or, as I preferred to believe, into a fairy princess.

Simmering with excitement I sat waiting my turn in the front row of the crowded hall. My father was seated on the platform beside the Purple Mother. Her hand was bedecked with rings. She fingered a medallion on her bosom which was clothed in purple. A scarf of gold tissue draped hair scraped from a low forehead to a top knot. She was an ageing Queen of Sheba. Dark eyes embedded in dusky cheeks, as restive as those of a bird and as wary, glanced furtively over the attentive faces of the audience. My father was her lean and hungry attendant. Behind the platform hung a huge photo of herself, her heavy jowled peasant's face garlanded with a wreath of white roses. Below it was a banner embroidered with the theosophical symbol of interlaced triangles encircled by a serpent swallowing its tail.

After my father had opened the meeting with a eulogy on Blavatsky as the Founder of the T.S., including appreciation of Madam Tingley's contribution to her work, it was his duty as chairman to call on each of those in the audience chosen to contribute to the programme.

When it came to my turn I knew by the way he ran a hand through his hair, cleared his throat, avoided my eyes, that he was more nervous on my behalf than I was for myself. Determined not to let him down, I boldly mounted the platform, executed a sweeping curtsey to the Purple Mother which aroused a murmur of approval from the audience, and announced with great aplomb that I was — The Spirit of Nature.

'All day long I am creeping close to the earth and the fresh spring grass,' I continued in clear, ringing tones. And since I recited the whole of the nonsense verse without having to be prompted, suiting gestures to fit the words, my performance was greeted with a thunder of applause which brought colour to my cheeks, sparkle to my eyes.

'Sweet', 'charming', were the adjectives wafted to me on the platform. I was on top of the world. But the crowning glory was the laurel wreath the Purple Mother accorded me. She remarked to my father that he had every right to be proud of a little daughter who had obviously a talent for acting that would be well worth cultivating. I danced away in a blaze of light to a rosy future, of which my dainty frock was to be a sad reminder in days to come. It was the only occasion in New York on which I brought credit rather than disgrace on my parents.

3   Negro Friends

I don't believe my parents realized what it would mean to their Irish daughter to be obliged to attend an American Methodist School. Their theosophical beliefs may have made them insensitive to class distinctions. My mother just considered herself a cut above her neighbours and kept, as she boasted, to herself, and left it at that. Her isolation prevented her mixing with the many nationalities congregating in our part of New York. To most of them the poor Irish were almost as much a depressed class as the negroes. As for me, I trod upon the shadow of a German, a Jew, Italian or Latvian without being able to distinguish one from the other. They were all Americans to me. My parents doubtless considered I would receive a better education at a Church School, for a modest fee, than I would in a crowded class at a State School. I'm sure they were mistaken. At this school I suffered an eclipse that might have been total had I not somehow fought back.

I was at a disadvantage at the outset by being dressed differently from the other children. Instead of appearing triumphantly at school in a new rig-out, I was obliged to wear mother's cast-offs, which she had painstakingly altered and cut down to fit me. She was no expert at the job. I must have looked very odd.

They started in on me as soon as I appeared in the playground. The abuse I shouted at my tormentors in an Irish accent proved an added source of mirth. I was obliged to share a desk with a little bully whose red hair reminded me painfully of Jasper Lindsay. In return for the paper pellets he kept flicking in my face when the teacher's back was turned, I hit out at him with the same ferocity I'd used on Jasper. I was hauled in front of the class and ordered to stand in a corner with my pinafore over my head for the remainder of the morning — doubly humiliated by the injustice of it.

Mother said that two wrongs don't make a right. I was as much to blame for striking the boy as he was for provoking me. Once I had settled down and had begun to make friends I'd enjoy school. I didn't think so.

The scripture lessons were the high-water mark of the day. I was itching to be asked to tell a Bible story in my own words. I longed to shine. Yet should the Headmistress, who took scripture, ask me to repeat a text after her, the titter my accent aroused in the class shamed me into silence. So I met her commands with a stubborn refusal to open my mouth, and my punishment was to copy rows of pothooks and hangers on a slate in a desk by myself at the back of the class. Ostracized, mocked — a dumb Irish kid to my classmates, a backward child to my teachers — how could I have regarded that school except as an institution in which I was obliged to do penance for a sin I had never committed? I longed by some magic to change myself into a bird, free to fly over blue pastures; to be a fly on the wall or the janitor's cat, left to sun herself on the window-sill when I set off from the house in the mornings. I envied a tramp on the sidewalk at the end of 28th Street. But most of all I envied my brother for being too young to be sent to school.

After I had by chance discovered a negro quarter nearby, I took to streaking off, as soon as I was let out from school of an afternoon, to a street of mean shanties. Its dusty sidewalk was lined by tall sunflowers. To be accepted as an equal by the coloured children was a delight. For an hour or two each evening I discovered myself in them. The sun beat corrugated iron roofs into sheets of burning metal. Mangy dogs, which at first had greeted me with snarling barks, soon came to treat me as a friend. Dark-eyed women who had peered suspiciously at me through rents in ragged curtains, learnt to smile a welcome. Clothes of all colours hung out to dry in back yards where scraggy bantams pecked at the dirt. Mothers squatting on doorsteps, nursing their young at their breast, made room for me in their laps to console me as tenderly as they would one of their own children if I should hurt myself say in a vain attempt to imitate their children in turning somersaults. When I was comforted with a slice of juicy watermelon, I would dig my teeth into its pink flesh and spit the seeds at my playmates. I dreaded to see the shadows of my companions become less sharp, for it meant that the hour of departure had struck.

In vain did I try to keep my secret from the school kids. They tracked me down. Unthinkable to allow them to invade private ground! I fled. Stung by their shouts of, 'Irish pig, trash, dirty niggers' pal', I charged at them as blindly as a bull in a ring.

'You look a regular ragamuffin,' scolded mother. 'Where have you been to this hour?' I coughed up the truth.

Since mother as a theosophist subscribed to the brotherhood of man — irrespective of race, creed, colour or class — I don't believe she would have forbidden me to play with the negroes. I believe that her threat to fetch me from school, unless I returned home punctually for the tea each day, was prompted by the teacher, who had been informed by my tormentors that they had found me playing with negroes. With the desperation of a wild creature at bay I sought for a way out. I was aided by the leader of a gang which operated on the wasteland. Enrico, a swarthy, good-looking, Italian boy, whose toughness established his authority on the art of playing truant, was only too ready to initiate a novice.

On his instruction I set out each morning punctually for school, returned as punctually for tea, and managed to invent such a plausible account of the day's proceedings that it did not seem to occur to mother to doubt me or to carry out her threat. I even began to believe my own lies as readily as she did. As she didn't bother to check up on me perhaps she found lies more comforting than the truth.

At first I turned to the same negro quarter. The absence of the coloured children at school made the quarter less inviting, and I was wandering away disconsolately when the Tempter arrived in the guise of Enrico.

'What ye want to hang round them niggers for, kid?' he enquired derisively. 'White folks don't. See?'

I saw a raffish grin, a smudge across a cheek as dark as any coffee-coloured negro.

Enrico was my type. How could I resist his invitation to join his gang in Central Park? Off like a shot, I allowed him to haul me on to the back of a stationary lorry which was loading bales of goods from a neighbouring warehouse. Crouching with him under a tarpaulin that screened us from the driver we were soon miles from home. At an agreed signal I ran the risk of breaking my neck by jumping from the lorry on to Riverside Drive. His 'Buono, good for you, kid,' amply compensated me for the bad graze on my knee. I followed my leader to the park. Oh the joy of trailing over sunlit grass, in and out of the shade of blossoming trees, to a vast expanse of water, reflecting clouds sailing over lakes of blue!

Children of rich people, playing pussy games under the eyes of mother or of nursemaid, eyed us enviously as Enrico, producing an air gun, streaked past them to a shrubbery, with me tearing after him. We stalked our enemies strolling in the shade of paths that led to the wild part — to me it seemed open country. Descending with a whoop on the gang engaged in playing cowboys and Indians, Enrico claimed his right as chieftain. To be accepted as his squaw by the little band crowned me with a glory which blinded me to the danger of joining in their further adventures. I took part with them in their reckless raids on fruit stalls. No scruple prevented me snatching an apple or a pear and making off with it.

The ugly word thief was not in my vocabulary. I was merely taking part in a risky game, in which my skill earned the approval of my comrades. A sweet shop with candies on the counter was our Cockaigne. We hunted in couples. One would stand guard, while the other, armed with a dime against detection, would make a grab at the counter, and, streaking out like lightning down the street, would share his booty with the gang round the corner. Should we come across a Cop on the prowl we'd disperse. But retribution awaited me. Waylaid on my return from a sortie by a classmate who asked why I had been absent from school for the last couple of weeks, I told a blatantly foolish lie. I said my brother had the measles, and the doctor had forbidden me to return to school until the danger from infection was over. But she squealed on me.

My mother looked grim when she met me at the door next day.

'Your sins have found you out, Miss,' she said, propelling me indoors. 'Give an account of yourself. Where have you been?'

This time I told the truth and said I had been playing with children from the wasteland in Central Park.

'As far from home as Central Park when you should have been at school,' she wailed. 'I despair of you. And to think I've been fool enough to believe that you were mastering your multiplication tables, learning the alphabet, and all the other tall tales you have made to deceive me! You deserve a thrashing. I'm at my wits' end to know how to deal with you.'

I faced her anger with the indifference of a sinner; indeed welcomed it as my deserts. But when she announced that her first duty was to inform my Headmistress, who had written blaming her for failing to report a case of measles in the family, in proof of which she demanded a doctor's certificate, I broke down. Sobbing hysterically I begged and implored her to punish me as she thought I deserved, but not to send me back to school.

'Go to your room,' she ordered, 'and stay there.'

The climax came next morning. My father was with the Purple Mother in California. Without him there I had to rely on my wits and perfidy. Both failed. Mother took me to school herself. I tried to foil her by sneaking from the cloakroom as soon as her back was turned. Grabbing me, she marched me straight down the corridor stinking of disinfectant to the Headmistress's room. Handing Miss Houston a note which she said explained the situation, and promising in future to fetch me from school, she abandoned me.

I always feel vulnerable in the presence of officialdom. My heart bright and hard as a bead, I watched the figure as erect as a Grenadier Guard reading the closely written page. Roses on her desk blotted out the disinfectant. I lowered my eyes to their replica on the hearthrug. She said my 'disgraceful conduct' deserved the cane, and ordered me to take off my coat and hold out my hand. I obeyed with a speed that seemed to disconcert her. Taking a cane from the drawer, she held it between her hands like a ruler; dallied with it. I supposed it part of my punishment to be kept waiting with outstretched hand for a lash. The thought of boasting about my courage to Enrico lessened the suspense.

'I guess,' she reflected, eyeing me shrewdly, 'I should make an example of you by caning you in front of the class. It will be a warning to others who may take it into their heads to act as you have and teach you a lesson you're not likely to forget.'

She commanded me to follow her, but I stood my ground.

'No,' I cried. 'No.' With the ferocity of a wild cat I turned on her, sprang from her grasp, knocked over a chair and flung myself on the floor. Righting the chair, she leant over me to haul me to my feet. I thrust a booted foot into her groin with such force that she backed, wincing. Quick to take advantage of her recoil, I gave her a further kick that sent her reeling against the desk. White to the gills, panting, she raised a threatening arm ready to deliver a lash of the cane. I turned over, and burying my face in the rug, offered her my buttocks. She struck ferociously, but the layers of underclothes mother insisted I should wear buffered the sting of the cane.

It was not pain that set me sobbing. It was degradation. She summoned my teacher.

'Tell Miss Taylor to come to me immediately. This child is totally unfit to mix with normal children. She must be expelled forthwith.'

Although her words resound through the years, they had little meaning for me. I clung in desperation to the leg of the desk, for fear my teacher would try to take me to the classroom. It must have looked like a ragged bundle she was commanded to remove from under the desk. I was the worst case of delinquency that had been at the school within her knowledge. Could it have been sympathy I detected in Miss Taylor's mournful, dark-rimmed eyes, as she wiped my blotched and tear-stained face with her own handkerchief?

She handed me over to the caretaker with a note from Miss Houston, asking my mother to call on her after school.

Mother examined the marks on my behind more in sorrow than in anger. She said, with a sardonic twist of her lips, that my father would be none too pleased to hear that his daughter was only fit for a Reformatory.

Leaving us children to the care of the janitor, she set off for the fray. She wasn't going to let me down this time. In her opinion a mistress who had to use corporal punishment to enforce discipline was better suited to be the warden of a penitentiary than the Head of a Church School.

As though to prove myself a prophet, I caught the measles. Ronald caught it from me, and as the trees in the park were stripped of their autumn splendour we were both stuck away in a bedroom steeped in a perpetual twilight by the newly completed block of flats.

On a sunny morning not long after we had recovered I came into the living room in search of my brother to find him leaning out of the open window, his head and shoulders silhouetted against a luminous sky. By his elbow on the windowsill lay what looked like a hedgehog, but which on coming closer, I saw was a clot of sticky burrs he had gathered from the wasteland. Intent on using the burrs as missiles to aim at the janitor's little daughter in the area below, he did not notice that I had crept up behind him, with the intention of joining in the sport. As I grabbed the burrs, he raised his knee to the sill, and with a piercing scream toppled out head first.

Whether I had accidentally knocked him in an effort to reach the burrs, or he had lost his balance, I shall never know. Looking back on it I think that I may have given him a shove. Instead of running to fetch my mother I stood stock still on the spot from which I had seen him vanish, unable to believe that he would not pop up again, like a jack-in-the-box, at the open window. Amongst the voices which reached me from the area I recognized an agonized wail from my mother. A minute later she thrust a panic-stricken face in at the door.

'Were you in here when Ronnie fell?' she demanded. 'Have you lost your tongue? Answer me.'

I nodded assent. 'Then why on earth didn't you warn him not to lean so far out of the window?'

Before I could reply to a question I could not answer, she dashed from the room to meet a little procession of neighbours entering the hall.

Like a funeral procession crossing a stage, I watched from the room the janitor, my brother lying limp in his arms, a bruise the size of a duck's egg gleaming on his deathly white forehead, followed by my mother and a couple of women. They were carrying Ronald to my parent's room. I thought he was dead.

Stricken with grief for the loss of a brother I both hated and loved, it was not for me to take part in the unusual commotion that went on in the flat for the remainder of the morning. During the scurrying to and fro of neighbours, the arrival and departure of a doctor, the sudden appearance of an iceman tipping a huge block of ice into the sink, I remained alone and forgotten. Mother came bustling into the room, a rent sheet in her arms. I thought it odd — since I knew the dead to be colder than ice — that she should bid me fetch her workbasket and help her tear the sheet into strips. The janitor's wife had offered to make bags to hold the ice which the doctor had ordered to be bandaged to Ronald's head. To hear that he was to be kept perfectly quiet in a darkened room with ice packs to his head until the doctor called again released the steel band which seemed to be clasped across my chest. Scalding tears mingled with hysterical laughter.

'No need for you to fret,' she said. 'If all goes well, Ronnie should be up and about again by the end of the week.'

Strictly forbidden to disturb my brother, I once permitted myself to peep into my parents' room. Propped up by pillows, in bed, his head swathed in bandages, he was gorging himself on ice-cream. His eyes, pin-pointed by light from the window, rested enquiringly on mine for an instant.

No more delicacies for either of us, once my father returned from his travels. He had been dismissed from the service of Katherine Tingley and there was no money. An early fall of snow turned the waste land into a pleasure ground for winter sports. The whiteness and silence of the snow shed a beauty on even the meanest things, changing distant buildings into crystal palaces, which at night were encrusted with jewels. Outdoors came indoors. Our boots let in the wet and mother could not afford to have them mended. Huddled in our overcoats in an effort to keep warm once the heating had been cut down to save fuel, our faces glued to the window, we watched others more fortunate than ourselves erect a snowman on a rubbish dump, or engage in a battle of snowballs. When we complained about the diet of maize porridge and milk we were told we should be thankful to have anything to eat. We often went to bed hungry. Lying awake, my tummy rumbling, I kept an ear cocked to follow the disputes between my parents about the rights and wrongs of the disaster which had happened with the Tingley lady.

'You must have known,' I heard mother scold, 'that by siding with Annie Besant against Purple, you were putting a nail into your own coffin. That old autocrat can stand no rival. She and Besant are at daggers drawn. You knew well enough when you went with her to Point Loma that her intention was to found a Headquarters that was to rival that of Annie Besant's at Adyar. Yet you were fool enough to cross her. Here have I been left for months to cope with quarrelsome and ailing children, skimping and scraping to make ends meet, and you away sunning yourself in California — living on the fat of the land I'll be bound. With no money coming in, and no prospect of getting any as far as I can see, it means that we shall have either to beg or starve.'

Father chided her. He had stood by a principle and the angels were on his side.

4 The author's mother and father, as she remembers them in her hey-day

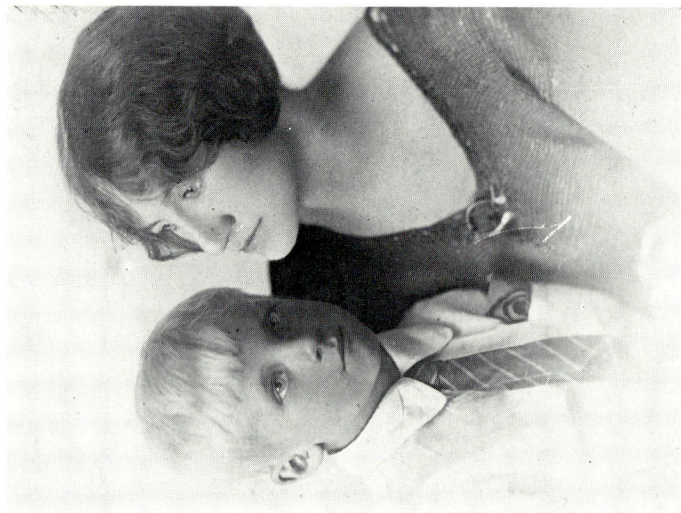

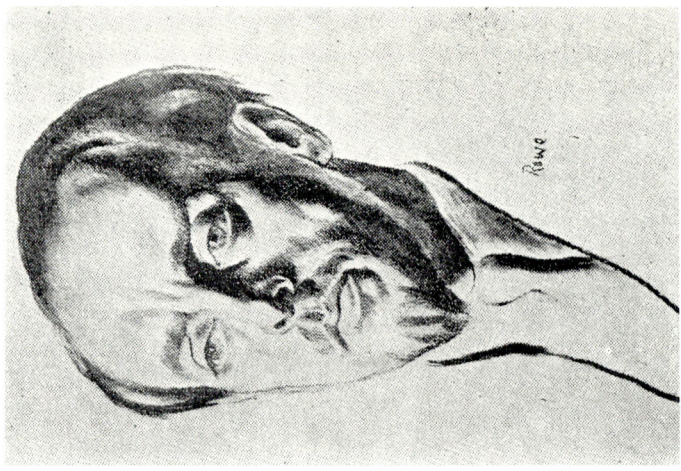

5 (*left*) A photo taken in
Melbourne of the author
and her son Michael at
the age of eight
(see p. 116)

6 (*right*) Sketch of
Gibson Young by Rowe

Such disputes went on every day. When father reminded mother that she must take the rough with the smooth, she'd respond, her cheeks flaming, that she had taken more than her fill of the rough. Who was going to have the children's boots soled and heeled? Or pay the arrears of rent? His head was in the clouds, and he had better come down to earth.

His feet, he assured her blandly, were firmly planted on the earth. He hadn't travelled the length and breadth of a great country without keeping his eyes and ears open. He had wasted his talent on a set of nincompoops in the Theosophical Society for too long. Now that he was no longer at the beck and call of a petty-minded, jealous woman, he was free to try his hand at journalism. He had a letter of introduction to the editor of the *New York Times*. If nothing came of that, he had other staunch supporters in the Society who would be willing to help.

'Cheer up, Ellie,' he encouraged, patting her cheek, 'the prospects are not so dark as you've painted.'

The turning point came at Christmas. Having followed my parents' troubles I was able to make the best of it when I found nothing in my stocking on Christmas morning. Why should I complain when (as father took great pains to remind us at breakfast) the Christ child whose birthday we were supposed to be celebrating had been born in poverty. As though to applaud these fine sentiments and my stoic resolution the doorbell rang. 'The postman!' we shouted in chorus. Ronnie and I rushed to the door. Nothing on the mat. But on the landing outside there was a hamper, delivered to our door by a messenger in the chocolate livery of the Waldorf Hotel.

'Dunlop?' he enquired, grinning at our gasp of surprise. Our delighted cry, 'A present from Father Christmas', brought our parents out. 'The Gods,' said father, consulting the label, 'are looking after us. Their name is Adela Stern.'

It took all our efforts to drag the gift indoors. We hovered over its contents. Mother was the first to swoop. She pounced on an envelope amongst the packages wrapped in fancy paper, tore it open and held before my father's astonished eyes a cheque for a hundred dollars.

'Didn't I tell you,' he said, 'we had a staunch friend in Adela Stern? She sure has done herself proud.'

'And all for the love of you,' said mother. 'Once our debts are paid off, we can hold up our heads again. Maybe our luck has turned. Perhaps some of those articles you've sent round may be accepted.'

'It takes another woman's belief in me to restore yours,' he teased.

After dinner, father, mellowed by wine, smoking a fat cigar, described himself as a boy running barefoot over the hills and shores of Arran before he had lost his first love when his mother died. It was easy enough to believe — his blood ran in my veins too — that he had been driven by the strictness of his fanatical father to leave his home in Ardrossan at the age of fourteen to fend for himself in the slums of Glasgow.

'Is it holding yourself up as an example to your children you are? Or is it praising yourself?' mother rebuked.

'It is better,' he retorted with pardonable pride, 'to rebel against tyranny than to submit to it. But he who takes the law into his own hands must abide by the consequences — as my little daughter knows to her cost.'

I guessed by his benign smile that he at least pardoned my conduct. I felt very grateful.

He had never regretted that he had to earn his keep as errand boy to a newsagent's, nor that he had been forced to educate himself. He had spent the extra money he made by doing a paper round each morning on battered editions of the classics — both poetry and prose — he picked up secondhand on bookstalls. His favourite was philosophy. He had permanently weakened his eyesight by poring over Plato, Plotinus, Aristotle, and particularly the work of the slave, Epictetus, by the light of a tallow candle smuggled into his attic room. Plotinus had paved the way to theosophy; the theory held by Pythagoras of the transmigration of souls to his belief in reincarnation. Already at fifteen he had been preparing to meet Blavatsky.

An identification disc of an indelible and astral blue that he wore on his hand to his grave distinguished it from that of all other men. It came from his boyhood in Glasgow. At his request and for the price of a pint, a dock labourer who did tattooing had imprinted a circle about the size of a sixpence on the back of his hand at the base of his thumb.

An article of his that did finally appear in the *New York Times* attracted the attention of George Westinghouse, the founder of the firm bearing his name. I have a vague idea that it dealt with the relation of publicity to the expansion of the electrical industry; a theme poles apart from theosophy, but one near to the heart of Mr Westinghouse. He summoned my father to an interview.

We sat at tea waiting for his return. 'Your father has been a long time gone. What can be keeping him?' mother repeatedly enquired of the clock.

When he did appear, as hilarious as though he had been celebrating, she eyed him as though she suspected infidelity.

'Well, out with it,' she snapped. 'What happened?'

'I come with good tidings. *Henceforth I ask not good fortune. I, myself, am good fortune,*' he quoted from Whitman.

The result of the interview had exceeded every expectation. This hard-headed businessman had been so impressed by what he had been pleased to call his novel ideas that he was willing to give him a chance to put them into practice. He invited father to join the publicity department of British Westinghouse, not in America but in London.

'Now perhaps my sceptical wife believes in her husband?' he asked.

'I do indeed,' she assured him vehemently. Her periwinkle blue eyes swam with tears. 'Forgive me for doubting you. I take back all I said.'

The warmth of their embrace left me out in the cold.

Our days of tribulation were over. Mother began making plans. It wouldn't do to travel on a luxury liner — the expense of which was to be deducted on easy terms from my father's salary — looking like scarecrows. We should need new clothes for the voyage. The sale of our few sticks of furniture would have to cover the cost of replenishing a scanty wardrobe.

For me the knowledge that I was to be separated from my family on arriving in London spoiled the pleasure of leaving. I thought it grossly unfair that I should be sent off, although in the care of my father, to an unknown aunt in Ireland, while my brother was to be kept like a lamb with my mother. It sickened me. I drooped. An attack of gastric 'flu forced mother to abandon her packing in favour of me.

I look upon our exile in New York with no pleasure. That prosperous city is to me a necropolis, its skyscrapers catacombs, a wasteland in which I only survived because I had some of the hardiness of a weed.

4 Killiney Hill

No strange aunt comes to take me from my father on the night the mail boat from Holyhead docked at Kingstown. The impossible happens. My grandfather trudges to meet me, trailing his ashplant behind him, a rain-laden wind in his face. I come, like a sea bird, to rest in his arms. I am his sweetheart, his pet, his bird, and in my new reefer coat with gilt buttons to match the braid, I am his yankeydoodle too. A tear drips from the tip of his nose in gratitude for my safe return. The doors of a house, stone grey, solid and foursquare, facing a green valley bound by the sea are open to welcome me.

After the night birdsong awakens me to sunlight. At the sound of a rake on the gravel drive I spring from bed, and am dressed and out of the house in a twinkling to join my grandfather. Crisp, white curls hang down from under the brim of a battered felt hat; shaded from the strong light are eyes as blue as the sky, in cheeks as red as an apple. He is digging pancakes of cowdung he has collected from the neighbouring fields in his wheelbarrow into the soil at the foot of the stakes to nourish his sweetpeas. His sweetpeas are the best in all Ireland. Have I ever heard that the scent of sweetpeas keeps flies from a room? He'd be happy to have his remains used to manure a cabbage patch. Cemeteries, in his opinion, should be turned over to the use of market gardeners.

My three years away have dug deeper furrows in my grandmother's brow; otherwise she is unchanged. Blue veins are knotted in hands like withered leaves. At breakfast, she has only to nod for me to scrape a bowl of 'stirabout' clean. My grandfather and I play a game of makebelieve. To induce me to eat a new-laid egg which I don't like, he mixes its contents in a cup with sugar and breadcrumbs, turns it out on a plate, and offers me a haystack from the newly-mown meadow adjoining the house. A bunch of cherries hanging from a stick over the mantelpiece are the drops of blood he has drawn from the backside of a rascal he caught helping himself to his crop. The priest we see climbing Killiney Hill to the village, his soutane flapping like black wings, is a wily old jackdaw. Granny disapproves of him ridiculing priests. Every man is entitled to worship God as he thinks fit. As a Quaker, a member of the Society of Friends, she does not hold with the Catholic religion, but she respects those who do. Even a lapsed Catholic like my grandfather should be tolerant to those who have remained loyal to their faith.

My grandfather grunts.

'It used to make my blood boil,' he says to me on the quiet, 'to see those priests, beyond there in Tipperary, where I was born, fleecing the poor to feather their nests.'

He'd flourish his ashplant, and turning to me belligerently ask who gave the Church a monopoly of God? Organized religion was a racket that Christ Himself would have been the first to deplore. Those fine 'boyos' in Dublin who clamour for Home Rule were ready enough to place themselves under the yoke of Rome. Patriots who laid the blame for Ireland's poverty at England's door would do well to remember that Parnell was hounded to his death by the self-righteous hypocrisy of the priests. He'd as lief have Ireland ruled from Whitehall as he would from the Papal See.

His ranting meant little to me except that I was flattered to be treated as an adult.

The Peak — set back in its own grounds from Killiney Hill, its front windows reflecting dawn and sunset on Dublin — did not in fact belong to my grandparents. It was run by my Aunt Louisa as a Nursing Home for the old and ailing, some of whom my grandfather described as 'not quite right in the head'.

'The fact is,' he said, 'that old house at Drumcondra was becoming too much for your Granny and me, and we're getting on in years. Your aunt advised us to sell out. With the proceeds and a mortgage we bought a property for your aunt large enough for her to set up in business on her own account, and to be a home for us for the rest of our lives. The Peak fitted the bill. Your aunt fell in love with it as soon as she set eyes on the view from the front. She is qualified for the job by her years of experience at the best hospital in Dublin. Her success at The Peak is partly due to the high opinion the doctors at St Patrick Dunn's have of her work.'

The green baize door, which creaked back and forth on its hinges at all hours of the day, separated my grandparents' rooms from by far the larger part of the house devoted to my aunt's patients and her staff.

'Do as I do,' my grandfather advised. 'Steer clear of the patients. It's not for the likes of them to interfere with us, nor for us to trespass on their part of the house. Keep this side of the baize door. You have the run of Quarry Hill.'

Swing back a door in the yard and the gold of gorse and purple of heather shadowed by passing clouds is mine for the asking. If I risk getting my feet wet in the springy turf and avoid the precipitous dip of the quarry I can reach the sky that meets the brow. The Peak shrinks to a slate grey roof, a chimney, a spiral of smoke floating over a patchwork of sun and shade. Far off is a streak of blue for the sea. From a boulder I can see Kingstown Pier no larger than a raft. Toy ships are stranded in the sky. Below is Killiney village. On fine days bees plunder the honey-scented gorse. Quarry Hill gives without taking. To enjoy it was to know love without heartaches — an earthly paradise never since acquired.

Whatever I did I could not avoid the patients completely. I had come across Miss Archdale cruising about the countryside as aimlessly as a tramp. Until she revealed herself in the hall by taking off an old mackintosh and a weatherbeaten hat that she habitually wore pulled over her eyes I had taken her for a man. The mildness and melancholy of her watery blue eyes transfigured a face which, the hat gone, looked curiously naked. She blushed at my stare and asked my aunt who came down the stairs at that moment to introduce her to her niece, whom she had seen wandering like Alice in Wonderland over Quarry Hill.

Had I read that enchanting story? Upon my confessing, shyly, that I was unable to read, she promptly asked my aunt to give her the pleasure of letting her teach me. My aunt consented. She proved such a painstaking and patient teacher that reading came easily. She neither scolded for lapses of attention nor discouraged by faint praise. She was able to make printed words spring to life in the form of a visual image. I grew to be as fond of my teacher — clinically diagnosed, I was told later, as a manic-depressive with a tendency to suicide who, according to hearsay, owned an extensive property in County Kildare — as I believe her to have been fond of me. A thirst for learning in me complemented a need for affection in her. My aunt said that teaching me to read had done Miss Archdale more good than any treatment from her doctor.

If in Miss Archdale I found an ideal teacher, in old, bedridden, senile Miss Cudmore I found an ideal playmate. The once proud owner of a sheep station in New South Wales had no relatives left who cared a rap for her. She had been given into the care of my aunt by the Court of Chancery which administered her estate.

My aunt called her her 'baby'; she occupied the width of a double bed, had snow white hair, a complexion like marshmallow, and not a tooth in her head. When Aunt Louisa cuddled her, tickled her, pinched her cheeks, she would cackle and giggle with the delight of a two-year-old. Obstreperous and difficult when a nurse attempted to feed her, if my aunt held a feeding cup to her lips she would suck from the spout as contentedly as a child from a mother's breast.

'What is Tommy hanging round the door for I'd like to know,' she'd mumble to my aunt. 'He's been up to some mischief, I'll be bound. Tell him to come in, or clear out of that.'

I was reluctant to approach the bed. It smelled of stale urine. The old woman had a wild gleam in her china doll's eyes. Had my aunt not pleaded with me to humour her I might have continued to keep my distance. But once Miss Cudmore had hoisted herself up on the pillows and bid me saddle the bay mare, I could not resist joining in the game. It needed but for her to tug at invisible reins for me, at her bidding, to jump on the bed. Before my aunt left the room we were galloping in a mad race to the five mile paddock.

'That filly of yours, Tommy,' she'd say, 'ain't no match for the mare. Watch her. Don't she take that ditch like a bird?' Flourishing her whip, and flinging herself back on the pillows, she'd cry: 'Bail up, ye bitch. Bail up.'

'My,' she would chuckle, 'that was a near shave! We were within an inch of giving that old 'roo a kick in her pouch. Did ye see her make for the scrub?'

To the jingle of the bedstead's brass knobs, we'd jog up and down on our mounts through scrub to tracks between trees which Miss Cudmore said were blue gums in flower; clear a fence, and be off down a gully to shouts of 'Gee-up! Bail-up!' and shrill cries of 'Coo-ee!' I soon was as annoyed as Miss Cudmore if a nurse came in to spoil our ride. If Nurse Heiffernan, the beauty from County Down, scolded us for making a noise fit to wake the dead, Miss Cudmore would threaten to give her a taste of the whip. She of the milk and white complexion, raven hair and rosebud mouth was a hussy who larked with the drovers after dark. 'Mark my words,' she'd mumble out of the corner of her mouth, 'that one'll come to a bad end.'

Her malice, the spirit with which she enacted the escapades of her youth, made my return with her to the Australian bush the high watermark of the day.

Another woman had the ravaged beauty of a Byzantine madonna. She was shadowed by a nurse in the grounds of The Peak. I kept my distance from her. But she waylaid me one day in the hall when I came upon her unawares wringing her hands and with tears flowing down her pallid cheeks. I was making for the safety of the green baize door when she suddenly pounced on me, grabbed me by the hand, and, glancing about her furtively, dragged me into the privacy of her room off the hall. She closed the door and stood with her back to it. She had me trapped.

'Is it frightened you are of me, child?' she enquired. 'God is my witness, I'll do you no harm. It is not for the likes of me to touch so much as a hair of your innocent head.'

'Let me out. I've no right to be here,' I ordered.

'For mercy's sake, have pity on me,' she implored. Sinking to her knees, she raised eyes streaming with tears to mine. Intrigued to have a woman old enough to be my mother supplicating me on her knees, I asked what ailed her.

'I'm doomed,' she wailed. 'I have committed the unforgiveable sin, and am doomed to everlasting torment. Nothing can save me from the fires of hell.'

To have a grown woman grovelling at my feet and asking me to pray for her, though repulsive, also gave me a sense of importance. I asked her sternly what was the terrible sin she had committed.

Flinging herself into a chair, and rocking to and fro in fresh paroxysms, she sobbed, 'The sin against the Holy Ghost.'

Her mystifying disclosure aroused my curiosity. Before I could satisfy it, her nurse, a grim looking woman, as stiff as her starched cap and apron, marched into the room bearing her patient's dinner on a tray.

'Begone out of this,' shouted Mrs Mooney, threatening her with a clenched fist. 'You have no right to intrude.'

'Miss Fitzpatrick's niece has no right to be here, and you know it, Mam,' reproved the nurse.

My grandmother was my conscience. She made crooked paths straight. It was no hardship to come each evening before retiring to bed to kneel at her feet in the cosy firelit room to repeat the Lord's Prayer with her. Her knee was the altar at which I offered up a prayer to a loving and all-merciful Father in Heaven. With Mrs Mooney's confession in mind, I said I knew of one sin God would not forgive. She looked grave.

When she heard of my encounter with Mrs Mooney she blamed the nurse. Once before she had left her patient alone in the hall and had my aunt out scouring the district for hours in search of her. I was not to take to heart what a woman as ill as poor Mrs Mooney had said. She was suffering from delusions brought on by a mental disturbance following the birth of her younger son. She had two fine boys and a kind husband able to provide her with the best money could buy. All her troubles were brought on by herself. A lovely girl, she must have been lively too, and not at all the sort to be shut up in a convent. It was a great mistake on the part of the nuns to persuade her she had a vocation. They should have known better than to threaten her with the fires of hell. Maybe she thought that by refusing to take the veil and by leaving the convent to get married she had denied the will of God and therefore had committed the unforgiveable sin. Their teaching instilled into her at an impressionable age may have been responsible for her delusions.

Granny searched for a definition of delusion in the fire. 'A delusion,' she said, 'is a mistaken belief; one that has no foundation in fact; untrue, in the sense of being unreal.'

'Then what Mrs Mooney says about herself isn't true?'

'By no means. Pass me my spectacles. They're on the mantelpiece.'

Her Bible was kept ready to hand on a pedestal table at her elbow. By the light of the fire she read me the parable of the lost sheep. A spurt of flame from a sizzling coal lit up the cameo brooch fastening her shawl, the cleft in her chin, her fine and wrinkled cheek. A star shone in the intense blue of sky above the dark arbutus hedge. The green baize door creaked. The grandfather clock ticked loudly.

' "Verily, I say unto you",' she read, her voice rising like a song. ' "There is more rejoicing in heaven over one sheep that is lost and is found than of the ninety nine that went not astray." That is God's message to Mrs Mooney. Just as she would take her children in her arms to comfort them should they hurt themselves, even so is her heavenly Father waiting to comfort her. Let's go down on our knees and ask Him to lighten the darkness into which she has strayed.'

I was alarmed to see a tear trickling down her cheek on to the hand clasping the Bible.

I took the Bible from her and she opened dazed eyes. 'Help me back into the chair, like a good girl,' she whispered. 'I do be weary come nightfall.'

Her face was ashen. I settled her comfortably in the chair and asked her was she feeling unwell? Had she a pain? Should I call Aunt Louisa?

'You'll do no such thing,' she said testily. 'To be a burden to your aunt is the last thing I want. Kiss me goodnight.'

Her forehead felt damp to my lips.

Mrs Mooney and her delusions must have upset me more than I realized. I enjoyed being out in a drizzle of rain — what to the Irish is 'a fine soft day'. You could hear a mile off the bark of a dog, or the crunch of wheels on Killiney Hill or a train from Dublin steaming through Dalkey. So it was that I heard distinctly what a couple of women, leaning over the half door of their whitewashed cabins like a couple of old horses in a stable, said about me. I was passing through the village on my way to the back entrance of The Peak talking aloud to a doll made from a wooden clothes-peg I kept in my pocket.

'Mad as a hatter,' cackled the white haired old hag, wagging her head at me. 'Aye, to be sure, poor child,' replied her neighbour. 'It's a pitiful thing to see one so young afflicted. She's from the big house on the hill.'

To put as much distance as possible between myself and their cackle, I ran without stopping until I reached The Peak and rushed through the back door to collide with my aunt in the hall.

'I am mad,' I alarmed her by announcing. 'A woman in the village said I am.'

Clasping me in her arms, and tenderly stroking my damp hair, she bid me pay no heed to what a couple of ignorant old women had to say. They were a nasty, mischief-making lot down there. She'd had trouble with them before. I was by far the sanest, most sensible child she had ever come across.

Unconvinced, I explained that I talked aloud to the clothes-peg Granny had dressed for me.

And what more natural than for a child, without a playmate to talk to her doll? Hadn't she and my mother done the same when they were my age? She'd put on her hat and coat and go straight to the village to give those women a piece of her mind. I nevertheless avoided the village when out on my own, and threw the clothes-peg behind a boulder on Quarry Hill.

I was out on Killiney Hill on a cloudy day, ploughing through a drift of leaves, when at a turning of the road I came upon Mrs Mooney pinioned to an ivy-covered wall by her nurse.

'Let me go,' she shouted, thrusting her sleek bare head forward like a snake as though to spit venom in the face of her persecutor. 'I have a right to do away with myself if I wish.'

'Who gave you that right, Mrs Mooney?' I demanded to know. My voice startled her. She stared, glared, recognized me, and slumped against the wall as though winded. Meekly, she allowed the nurse to link her arm and me to take her hand. Muttering to herself that I am the spitting image of her son, Michael, she clung to my hand as to a life belt. She did not leave it go until she was safely anchored in a chair in her room.

Cunningly, she got rid of the nurse by asking her to fetch my aunt. No sooner was the door closed on her than she asked what had made me recall her to her senses out on the hill. Was I an emissary of the Holy Ghost — the Comforter? She searched my face with such hopeful intentness that to humour her and to seize the opportunity to deliver my grandmother's message of the love of God I said that perhaps I was. I repeated the parable of the lost sheep.

'I am the sheep that has gone astray?' she cried rapturously.

'Yes,' said I, quick as an evangelist to take advantage of her change of mood. 'And God is waiting to take you back to the fold.'

She believed me. Her brow cleared. Her muddy complexion took on a luminous transparency. Her eyes shone. The change I had made in her exalted me. I reminded her that her children needed her love as much as she needed the love of God. To do away with herself would be to commit the unforgiveable sin.

'Bless you, child, bless you,' she said, 'for the comfort you have brought to me this day.'

She had clasped me to her breast and was rocking me to and fro in her arms when my aunt appeared, the nurse at her heels.

'What's going on in here?' she scolded. Mrs Mooney turned to address her with new dignity. 'Kind as you have been whilst under your care, Miss Fitzpatrick,' she said, 'it is to your niece, God bless her, that I shall owe my recovery if by the Grace of God I recover sufficiently to return to my family. This little angel has, by the inspiration of the Holy Spirit, been the means of restoring me this day to my senses, to my peace of mind, and to the will of God.' I blushed with pardonable pride as she consecrated me a kiss on the brow.

My aunt, properly taken aback, decided to humour her. She said that with such a testimonial she would have no option but to buy me a cap and apron and take me on as one of her staff.

'Such a remark is unworthy of you,' rebuked her patient haughtily. 'I credited you with more perception.'

She showed a marked improvement from that day on. I attributed it to myself as much as to the efficacy of my grandmother's prayers. I was sometimes allowed to accompany her and her nurse on their daily walks. We robbed the hedgerows of foxgloves, of blackberries, of sloes. When she left The Peak, ostensibly cured, besides giving me a beautiful doll with real hair and eyes that opened and closed, she presented me with her mother-of-pearl rosary as a keepsake. My grandfather threatened that should he find me telling my beads, he'd throw the relic of popery on his compost heap.

The affection I received from those on either side of the green baize door made of that home of eccentrics, whether wrong in the head or not, a haven never equalled since. A bud such as I was could blossom there. To be wrenched from it by my parents was even worse than to have been wrenched away from them when I returned from America.

Mary, the housemaid, gave me the warning. I never entered the kitchen without being given a titbit such as a scone or jam tart hot from the oven. Cook had just handed me a tart, when in came Mary, white as a sheet, a shawl over her head.

'I'm after seeing the black coach this night,' she announced, 'and it careering down Killiney Hill, and not a soul in it to drive the horse.'

'Maybe it was the mist you saw rolling down the hill,' Cook suggested.

'Have I eyes in my head? I tell you I saw the coach as clearly as I'm seeing you this minute. It's a bad omen.'

'It is to be sure,' Cook agreed. 'I never heard tell of that hearse being seen without trouble is brewing. Let's hope it's for nobody in this house.' 'Amen to that,' said Mary, crossing herself.

My grandfather cut short our prayers that evening. He said he had a surprise for me, and had taken me on his knee when Aunt Louisa put her head round the door. She warned him that as I had a long day's journey ahead of me in the morning, she'd be back within half an hour to fetch me to bed. He nodded gravely.

'Well,' I said, pinching his chin, 'What's the surprise? Are you taking me to the Dublin Horse Show, as you promised? It's a long journey by tram. Perhaps we'd better go by train from Dalkey.'

'Make a clean breast of it,' advised Granny, shading the firelight from her eyes with a hand.

My parents, he began, clearing his throat, thought it high time their little daughter returned to the fine home they had prepared for her in London. My father was now on his way to Holyhead. I was to be ready to catch the mail boat with him at eight sharp in the morning.

'Enough,' I said, clamping a hand to his mouth. 'I don't want to hear any more. It's a joke.'

'It's no joke, Birdie,' he said, shaking his head. 'I'm in dead earnest.'

'But The Peak is my home. I have no other and you know it,' I protested shrilly.

If he had his way, he'd keep me with him till his dying day. 'Keep me, then, keep me,' I cried, clinging to his neck. Never had his cheeks, shiny from shaving soap, ruddied by the fire, his crisp white curls, his blue eyes misty with tears, been more dear. I clung to him desperately. No amount of assurance on his part — that my brother was longing for his playmate, my mother for her daughter, that his bird would return with the swallows in spring, that the doors of The Peak were ever open to welcome her—served to lessen the pain of leaving him, nor to stop my tears. I battled with my aunt, when she came to wrest me from his arms, as though fighting for my life.

'Go now, like a good girl,' he whispered in my ear. 'You're distressing your Granny, and she ailing.'

At the sight of her face pale with pain I slipped from his knee and was led, sobbing, to bed.

'My little daughter seems none too pleased to see me,' my father remarked wryly to Aunt Louisa at breakfast. 'I hope she's behaved herself?'

'Behaved is not the word,' my aunt assured him warmly. 'She

has been good as gold. There's not a soul at The Peak that won't miss her.'

He was glad to have such a fine testimonial to take back to my mother. As there were only a few minutes to spare before the jarvey arrived at the door, I'd best get the farewell to my grandmother over as quickly as possible.

Granny, decked out in best cap and shawl in honour of my father, sat propped up by pillows in bed. Her eyes lit up when I went in. She tried to smile. I ran to the bed, flung myself on her breast, and buried my face in her shawl. It smelt of mothballs. Her breast heaved. I looked up at her and she cupped my face in her hands and studied it as though to print each feature for ever on her mind.

'Your cap's crooked, Granny,' I said, setting it straight. She trembled. Her whole body trembled as though shaken by an ague. I asked if she were cold. She bit her lip and turned away her head.

'Don't forget,' I coaxed, 'I'll be back with the swallows.'

'Be a comfort to your mother,' she gasped, 'as you have been to me. And remember to say your prayers.'

At a call from my father, she clasped me so close that I could hear the irregular pound of her heart. 'I can bear no more. Go now,' she said, pushing me from her. She died of cancer a few months after I left The Peak.

5 Wandsworth

The new house was a little one in a dingy, suburban street, each house as like its neighbour as a pea. Ours was distinguished by a monkey-puzzle tree in the back garden — a Chile Pine which loomed like a gallows through fog in winter, and in summer shed no shade on the grass. In that house, guarded by the Chile Pine, I discovered a secret carefully withheld until my return from Ireland. In my absence, my mother had given birth to twins — a boy and a girl. The boy, born with a caul over his face, died after drawing his first breath. The girl, described as delicate, survived to become a potential rival for my parents' affections. Since we forget that which we don't wish to remember, all I do remember of Aileen as a baby is a frail looking little creature with mild blue eyes being rocked to sleep, over the fire, in my mother's arms.

I had learnt a thing or two in Ireland which stood me in good stead: that if I wanted to be liked I must strive to please, dissemble, conform to the demands imposed by others. Above all, my grandparents, my aunt and the patients had given me the confidence that I could be liked. I therefore became an apt pupil, a favourite of teacher and classmates alike, at the Board School, a barracks set in asphalt looking as forbidding as the one in which I had disgraced myself in New York.

Owing to Miss Archdale I was by far the best of my age-group at reading, a shining example to my cockney school fellows of how English should be spoken. To honour my grandmother I also took home all the prizes that were to be had for scripture. By the time an increase in my father's salary permitted him to move to a new house, its mock Elizabethan front facing the counterfeit wildness of Wandsworth Common, I had saved my parents the necessity of paying for my education by gaining a scholarship to a Secondary School.

Facts, such as dates of battles, reigns of kings, the boundaries of countries on maps or algebraic formulae or Euclidian puzzles and all other subjects in the school curriculum save English literature, had no effect on the self I kept to myself. They were temporary and useless baggage to carry around. The fourth form mistress, a lively, imaginative, fragile-looking woman like a harebell, had been sent to prison as a militant suffragette. She was able to share her enthusiasm for poetry with her pupils. She fired me with it so that when I sat for Matric I passed with honours in English. For Miss Marsden I thought I was ready to attempt anything. She put me to the test by asking me to distribute leaflets house to house for a suffragette meeting.

I wasn't ready. The leaflets I stuffed under the bed lay there until long after the date of the meeting. Dusty and torn, they reproached me for having betrayed the trust of someone who had the courage to lose her job and serve a six months' sentence.

For exchanges of confidence I looked to the servants whom we had by now. Eva came from an orphanage. She accepted the burden life had imposed on her without complaint. Her dark slits of eyes under her drooping lids, inflamed by ophthalmia, watered not with tears but from the drops put into them at the out-patients' department of an eye hospital on her afternoons off. She pretended to be outraged when, as a prelude to confiding in her that a sexual maniac had made an attempted assault on me on the way home from school, I asked had she ever seen a man with his fly undone. 'What do you take me for?' she asked indignantly. But her blush spoke for itself. I confessed I had. Where, when and how? She was all agog.

Taking a short cut from school that saved me a quarter of a mile through a lane at the back of some houses I had seen at dusk a man lurking by the hedge. I pretended to take no notice and summoning my courage made to pass him when he sprang out to make a grab at me. To my horror I saw something as red and raw as the entrails of a fowl protruding from his fly. Fortunately my satchel was crammed with books. I swung it from my shoulder and landed him a blow on the offensive object that sent him staggering into the hedge. Before he could recover I streaked like lightning to the main road and kept on running, without once looking back, until I reached our house.

Revolted by the glimpse I had caught of the man's exposed genitals, protruding like a huge snail from his dirty pants, I yet instinctively felt him to be a victim of some disease; and thinking that, somehow, I might have been infected I was ashamed to mention it to anyone but Eva. She made me promise not to take the short cut again without a school mate, or my friend, Mary Page.

Mary lived in a house that backed on to the railway line. The trains that rattled its windows smeared the panes with smoke. Mother would have considered their back parlour the last word in bad taste and she herself a lady compared with homely Mrs Page. When I went back with Mary to the door I was always asked to stay to tea and given a warm welcome by her mother.

Once Mary's nineteen-year-old-brother, Ken, honoured us with his company and after that I used to sit on tenterhooks waiting for his latchkey in the door. Should I catch him looking at me, I cupped my face in my hands to hide my blush. I dared not use the lavatory while he was around. I preferred to suffer rather than have him hear me pull the chain. I must have been either shy or vain, or both.

I was invited to stay a weekend with Mary. The pleasure of setting off in my Sunday best on a Saturday afternoon was spoiled by my having an obstinate pimple on my chin, which no amount of cream and powder could hide. Ken would be sure to notice. Even so I waited for him, seated on a black horsehair sofa, sweating in front of a roaring fire. The clock on the mantelpiece ticked away hours as I waited. I would have bitten my tongue rather than ask Mary when he was expected to turn up.

'If you two girls don't want to lose your beauty sleep,' said Mrs Page, plonking a supper tray on the table, 'it's time you were preparing for bed.' To postpone the hour, I made her stodgy homemade buns last as long as I could. To my relief Mary went first to the bathroom. By the time I joined her she was already curled up asleep in a double bed. I had started brushing my hair when I heard a brisk step that could only be Ken's mounting the stair. The footsteps paused outside our door. My heart leaped. There was Ken at the door.

'Hello,' he said in surprise. Nervously flicking his hair from his brow, he explained that he'd noticed a light under the door and he thought he'd have a word with Mary before going to bed.

I invited him in. He glanced at his sister. In the harsh raw light of an unshaded gas mantle her arm encircled a mass of dark curls.

A cat-like smile appeared on Ken's face. 'Maisie,' he said, 'would sleep if the house was on fire.' He closed the door quietly and planted himself on the edge of the bed. Producing a rosy apple from his pocket he polished it on his sleeve and offered me a bit. 'After you,' I said. Seated rigid at his side, I bit into his teeth marks and handed it back. 'You look different tonight. Your hair down suits you.' I thanked him for the compliment, saucily, blushing with pleasure. 'How old are you?' he asked. I added a year to my fourteen.

'You have a determined jaw for a girl of your age. I wouldn't like to get your monkey up. You've got —' he hesitated. I waited longingly for him to say sex appeal. 'Character,' he said. Disappointment struck me dumb. He munched the apple in silence, threw the core in the grate, and stretching his arms over his knees cracked his knuckles. The clean sweep of his jaw, the firm set of his lips, suggested a topic I hoped might keep him with me. I said that to judge by *his* jaw he should get what he wanted from life. He frowned. 'Not me,' he said gloomily. The necessity of earning his keep had driven him to take a job as a bank clerk. To rise from cashier to manager was the utmost of his ambition. A dull life but a safe one, it was good enough for him. But I thought, or perhaps hoped, that I detected despair in his eyes.

'You don't believe me?' he asked. Pleased by my definite 'no' he edged closer, peering into my face. I turned the full blaze of my eyes on him and then he put his arm around me. I felt I was offering myself, at any rate my disembodied self, to him. Mary stirred and turned over in her sleep. His 'Time all good little girls were in bed' brought me down to earth.

My imaginary romance collapsed at breakfast. There was no sign of Ken. Mrs Page said he had set off to meet his girl while we two lazybones were still in bed. If the rain kept off, and it looked as thought it might, he and Gladys intended to cycle to Box Hill. Fresh air fiends they were, those two. Never a fine weekend went by, but they were out scouring the country on their bicycles. She supposed it made up for having to be cooped up in a bank all week. Gladys was a typist in the same branch of Barclays as Ken. They had been keeping company regular for the last couple of months. Glad was the right girl for Ken: serious, hardworking, an honest-to-goodness, down-to-earth, kind of girl. No nonsense about her. As the information spilled out I cursed the retreating figure of Ken disappearing down some unknown road in sunshine with his right kind of girl. I left for home early and hurt.

Eva, raking out the kitchen range of a morning while the rest of the household drowsed comfortably in bed, was the alarm clock. I had a good half hour to get washed and dressed for school. When she was no longer there to give me a snatched breakfast I felt betrayed. My mother had summarily dismissed her for no fault of her own, as far as I could make out, except that she had been seen spooning on the Common with a soldier after dark. I told my mother she was entitled to her pleasures. My mother replied acidly that she was entitled to the fruit of them too. I did not know at the time that she had been pregnant. My ignorance of sex was almost complete.

Nancy blew into the house like a wind from her native Stockholm. Her predecessor crept about the house as though apologizing for being alive; Nancy blew and bounced. She had come to London to perfect her knowledge of English in order to help her fiancé. Hugo wanted to run a restaurant for tourists on the water front at home. In talking of Stockholm she became more alive than ever. Hands on hips, she'd thrust out her full breasts, glide over the kitchen linoleum, swish her wide cotton skirt, hum a tune, and be skating on ice with Hugo. Englishmen were dull. They didn't know how to set about courting a girl like the fellows back home. A head stuffed with book-learning was no good for a girl. Swirling me off my feet in her arms, she'd waltz me round the kitchen. Some day, some day, she'd sing, I'd be waltzing with boy friends in Stockholm. I must come to stay with her and Hugo after they were married. Through her eyes I saw a city glistening in snow like a Christmas card. A spire pricked a star.

She treated me like a younger sister. I should discard shapeless gym tunics and wear clothes that would show off my figure. She showed me how to use her curling tongs. I looked like a golliwog. She did her best to persuade me that breasts I thought too full for a girl were attractive to men. Men did not like flat chests. They liked a full bosom: her own for example. She'd have to show me how to make the best of myself.

'You don't think much of yourself, little Frükin. You think if you can't be attractive, you had better be clever. Ach! I blame your mother. If you've never seen yourself naked in a long glass, now is your chance.'

Hustling me, protesting, from the kitchen she propelled me upstairs to the wardrobe mirror in my parents' bedroom.

'What's the idea?' I asked.

'To see how sweet you are without your clothes. Undress. Look sharp. I'll keep watch on the landing, to warn you should your mother return from shopping.' The conventional respectability of an oak bedroom suite, a smooth white counterpane on the double bed, the intimacy of the pillows, accused me of trespass. The downcast eyes of Leonardo's feminine head of Christ from above the bed ignored the clothes that fell one by one at my feet. Not so the master alleged to have inspired the works of Madam Blavatsky. The glittering intensity of Koot Hoomi's eyes gazed at my nakedness with an embarrassing fixity.

I turned my backside to Koot Hoomi. Facing me in the mirror was my youthful body. I had never seen it full length before. I took pleasure in claiming it as my own. Daylight through the lace curtains glowed on tilted breasts, a rounded belly, lean thighs. I had raised an arm and was smiling through a cloud of hair at myself when Nancy bounced in. My mother had returned. Gathering my clothes in a bundle I shot upstairs to my own room to dress.

I plucked up courage to confess to Nancy my ignorance of sex. But I got nowhere because my brother returned just at that time from his Quaker Boarding School for the Easter holidays. What could she see in the tall lanky youth, stubble on his chin, a crack in his voice? She obviously preferred his company to mine. It was beyond my comprehension. I used to come upon them talking and laughing together in the kitchen and ignoring me.

'What you see in Ronald, beats me,' I said. 'He's so boring.'

'That's because you're his sister. I find him a charming boy, talented, an artist.'

She showed me with pride sketches he had made of her washing up at the sink. In a few lines he had suggested her snub nose, dimpled chin, the voluptuous curve of a breast in profile, a squiggle of curled hair.

'He hasn't flattered you,' I said, tossing the sketches at her. She snatched them possessively to her bosom, and eyed me contemptuously. My brother's talent was wasted on me. I didn't understand art.

Going upstairs one evening to fetch my French dictionary, I heard a murmur of voices coming from Nancy's room. The door was ajar. I pushed it open. Nancy, her bodice undone, a feverish sparkle in her eyes, her hair dishevelled, sat on an unmade bed, her arm round my brother's shoulder, his hand on an exposed breast. Two pairs of blue eyes met my astonished gaze for a moment in silence. 'Clear out,' he said. I closed the door with a shattering bang. Nancy was as sweet as pie to me next morning. I suppose she thought I'd tell.

I confided in Mary, not my mother. 'She must be hard up for a lover to try and seduce a school boy. I wouldn't mind betting she invented her Hugo,' was Mary's comment.

'She wears an engagement ring.'

'So could you,' remarked Mary dryly, 'if you bought one.'

We always had kippers for breakfast on Sundays. My father, in a blue dressing-gown, his hair still rumpled by sleep, unshaved, would be dispensing them as I entered the room dressed ready to attend a meeting at the local Friends Meeting House.

My head stuffed with dreams, I stuffed toast in on top of them, ear alert to catch snippets of conversation that might provide a clue to that part of my parents' lives closed to me. I had my doubts whether my father could honestly believe that Annie Besant and her eminent confederates in the Theosophical Society had actually discovered a world saviour in the Hindu youth — Krishna Murti. They had helped fate by sending him to Oxford to further his education in preparation for his role of saviour. The pity and terror which the story of the crucifixion never failed to arouse in me made their claim a sacrilege.

The Star in the East was set up as an organization within the Society to prepare the way for his mission. I regarded it already as a farce. It is to Krishna Murti's lasting credit that he had the good sense to repudiate Annie Besant's claim just at the critical moment when she was about to launch him on his public career as the new Christ.

I don't know to what extent my father was implicated in the Star in the East. I believe he attended meetings of the organization, and I understood him to have been impressed by the genuine spiritual quality of Krishna Murti. To my mother, he was the handsomest young man she had ever set eyes on, a worthy namesake of Krishna, the god.

Their talk of so and so having seen an auspicious aura around
the head of one of Besant's devotees — the self-styled 'Bishop'
Leadbeater who claimed to have receive messages from the
Masters who ruled over the destiny of mankind on the astral
plane — made me wince. Not that my father took such assertions
seriously. He spoke of them with a twinkle in his eye, a sarcastic
smile. But his willingness to associate with the credulous was
enough to make me critical of him.

Once a year when Grandfather Dunlop — whose religious
fanaticism had driven my father away from home — chose to
descend on our household there was no theosophical gossip over
the kippers. None of us dared touch a bit until he had bowed
his head in the silent grace habitual to Quakers. His presence,
like a Hebrew prophet or Michelangelo's God the Father,
dwarfed the rest of us. My father was at his most bland, mother
blusteringly self-conscious, my brother and I seen, not heard. On
his visits he used to attend the local Friends Meeting which, as
an elder in the Society, he was expected, if the Lord so moved
him, to address.

The table is cleared. The Common outside the casement window a blur of fresh green. My parents getting ready to attend
Meeting. I am deputed to bring Grandfather Dunlop his boots,
polished fit to see your face in by mother's own hands. He towers
above us. A beard as luxuriant as Tolstoy's sweeps his chest. I feel
myself blushing under his scrutiny. I hand him his boots.

'Your father's mother was just such a wee wisp of a thing as a
puff of wind might blow away as thou art, lass, when first I met
her.' Amazed by the unexpectedness of it I gape at him in silence.

'Aye,' he nods, 'and she was a saint. If ere she were missing
frae the house of an evening, I knew richt well she would be in
yon cave by the seashore on her knees in prayer. I canna' recollect
hearing a harsh word pass her lips. The folk back there in Arran
knew where to come for comfort in tribulation. The Lord knows
His own.' He sighed, his eyes growing moist as he gazed into the
green haze of the Common. 'He took her to Himsel' when your
father was no higher than yon table. A great sorrow it was to be
sure.'

I ventured to remark that my father ran away from home when
he was fourteen. His bushy brows set in a beetling frown.

'Aye. A thorn in the flesh was Daniel, to me and to the guid,
God-fearing woman I took to mother him in place of her who

had gone. He wouldna pay heed to a word his stepmother said. An obstreperous, wilful lad was your father in his youth. Many's the time I had to take the rod to him.'

' *"Lead a child in the way he should go, and when he is old he will not depart therefrom,"* says the Scriptures. He took it badly that I sought to chastize him for his guid.'

'Dinna forget, lass,' he said as he rose to his full six feet from lacing his boots, 'that ye have the blood of a saintly grandmother in thy veins. If thou favour her in righteousness thou shalt not go far wrong.'

In obedience to a common impulse all heads turned to look at the rugged countenance of my grandfather as he rose to address those who had waited for the Spirit to move him in the simplicity of the Quaker Meeting House.

' *"I have sought for my Beloved behind lattices."* ' It soon became evident that my grandfather was not referring to the Highland lass — his first love — whose likeness he had traced in me, and whom I now imagined speeding from a cave along a seashore at sundown to escape an incoming tide. He spoke of the Beloved of King Solomon: *The Rose of Sharon,* the *Lily of the Valley,* the Beloved, whom all men seek, the incarnate Godhead hidden in the secret depths of the soul. Such was his interpretation of the Song of Songs. I thought it odd that he, who spoke so eloquently of love, should have dealt so harshly with his son.

None who heard him on that Sabbath morning delivering his message to the Friends could have foreseen that, when as white and stricken in wits as Lear, he should have died blaspheming the name of the very God he had worshipped.

6 Killiney Again

In that most perfect, last, unforgettable summer before the First World War as a reward for passing Matric I was given a month's holiday at The Peak.

In a shirt blouse tucked into the waist of a full skirt, worn ankle length (girls' legs, in those days, were to be imagined, not seen), a straw boater tilted rakishly on hair tied at the back in a large bow, I went down the gangway of the mail boat into the arms of Aunt Louisa. She was not alone. Her escort, as elegant in tweed as an advertisement for a tailor, a tall, distinguished-looking man, raised his trilby when introduced as Mr Emerson. My aunt's coquettish smile betrayed her interest in him. He was an Indian Civil Servant at home on leave who had been advised by his doctor to take a rest cure at The Peak.

It was a shock to find that the entrance hall looked surprisingly small, the staircase much less imposing, all the old patients gone. The green baize door had gone. 'No need for it now,' my aunt explained, heaving a sigh from a bosom upholstered in tawny silk. 'You won't recognize Granny's room. I've changed it to suit myself.' She showed me into a bright little boudoir, its couch and chairs upholstered in a gay flowered cretonne, muslin curtains catching the sunlight that wavered on walls tinted cream, a crimson carpet on the floor of what had once been the dingy little parlour to which I had come to say prayers at my grandmother's knee.

The sole monument to her piety was the pedestal table by the hearth on which, to have it ready to hand, she had kept her Bible. The bowl of sweetpeas reminding me of my grandfather filled me with remorse.

My aunt eyed me anxiously. Did I think it heartless of her to have banished all trace of my grandparents? On the contrary, to have transformed the room so that she could use it without being continually reminded of the past was the most sensible thing she could have done. If I looked upset it was because the sweetpeas reminded me of Grandpa saying their scent kept flies from a room.

'It does. I've proved it,' she said. 'No sweetpeas we've had since equalled his.'

I felt too ashamed to confess that I had refused his last request. It happened like this. When I was fourteen and he was over eighty, he had made a trip from Dublin to spend a summer holiday with me and my family at Llandudno. He had aged greatly since I had clung to his neck, sobbing my heart out at the thought of leaving The Peak. Mother complained that he had grown so deaf she had to shout herself hoarse to make him hear. It bored me to have to sit talking to him in a shelter on the promenade when I was aching to join a group of boys and girls on the beach. On the evening before he was to leave for Dublin he asked me to take a stroll with him, for old times' sake, around the Great Orme. I said I couldn't.

'Why not?' he enquired.

'I have a date.'

'What's that you say?' he asked in bewilderment, cocking a hand to his ear. I shouted at him that I had arranged to meet a boy friend on the pier.

He eyed me shrewdly. 'You're young to be courting,' he said, and turned on his heel.

It brings a lump to my throat when I think of him — a lonely old man, bent with age, trailing his ashplant on the gravel drive, rejected by the grand-daughter he had loved. He didn't go by himself around the Great Orme.

Whilst climbing Killiney Hill to The Peak on a blustering autumnal day he fell to the ground with a haemorrhage on the brain. My aunt wrote that as he did not regain consciousness it was the death her dear father would have chosen for himself.

It didn't take me long to realize that my blue eyes were a magnet for staid Mr Emerson. So apparent was it that I expanded in his presence like a Japanese paper flower in water. I began to play-act. I danced through meadows of seeding grass to Dalkey's strand shadowed by my grave cavalier for a dip in the blue sea.

I played on his susceptibilities all I could; allowed remarks I considered clever to fall readily from my lips. A knowledge of Hindu beliefs gleaned from my father enabled me to expound the doctrine of reincarnation and *karma*. I tore down his defence of the caste system with a revolutionary's zeal. He told my aunt I was a gifted, brilliant girl who should be given the advantage of a university education.

Dinner in the evening was by candlelight. It was attractive to youth, to age and to every fluttering night insect, especially moths, which flew through the open window to their death. In an effort to rescue one of them my hand accidentally grazed Mr Emerson's. A thrill ran up my spine. And when he took the opportunity of my aunt's absorption in carving a leg of lamb to link my little finger in his and hold it as though encircling it with a ring, gazing ardently at me while he did so, the blood inflamed my cheeks and set my heart racing. I could hardly breathe and remained dumb for the rest of the meal. Aunt Louisa thought it was because my month's holiday was nearly over. As a treat, before I left The Peak, she suggested the three of us should take a trip to Glendalough — a beauty spot in the Wicklow Hills. We should hire a jaunting car for the day, picnic by the lake, have tea at the hotel, and return in time for an evening meal. It would be something for me to remember. Mr Emerson thought it a splendid idea; but when he looked at me for confirmation, a maidenly shyness, a bashful blush, showed I wanted more of what caused the blushes.

The lough was set in purple hills. The water, black as ink below, crystal clear in the hand, tasted acrid like the lees of wine. I shared my aunt's side of the jaunting car on the way to the lake and shared, at his instigation, Mr Emerson's side on the way back.

In the violet hour when bats trace their blind way over darkening hedgerows, when birds dart to nests, and sunset fades to aquamarine, I was tucked cosily in a rug, cradled in my admirer's arm. Each jolt of the car, as the horse, to the flick of the jarvey's whip, trotted nimbly through lanes sweet-scented with honeysuckle and mown hay, brought my head closer to his heart. Mr Emerson spread the rug cunningly. Only my head could have been visible to my aunt. When she, to arouse my attention, pointed out a landmark, Mr Emerson warned her that I had fallen asleep. A lecher? Then I was a wanton. Secretly, under cover of the rug, I assisted his fingers to unbutton my blouse. A budding breast flowered in his hand.

Anyone who has felt sexual excitement on a train journey can understand the effect each saw of the jaunting car, as it rounded a curve, or lurched over a rut, had on us. We were locked in a discreet but voluptuous embrace. The colder his hand became the warmer my breast, soft, I thought, softer than a rose. My limbs, my whole body, ached deliciously for some excess. I prayed that the car ride might never come to an end. It came just as his lips had closed over mine.

'The lights of The Peak are in sight,' said my aunt. Wrenched apart, I opened my eyes to the stars. The expression in Mr Emerson's eyes, as he helped me to alight, the possessive grip of his hand on my arm, scared me. I decided I had gone too far.

Pleading fatigue, I made a bolt for my room, locked the door, and as a defence against him whom I had brazenly encouraged, kept it locked at night for the rest of the week.

I believe it was as much to celebrate the relief of my departure as her birthday that my aunt threw a party on the night before I left The Peak. I suspect also that it was to rival Mr Emerson that she insisted on inviting a set of medical students from Trinity. I complained that I had nothing suitable to wear. So she produced from her wardrobe a black velvet gown that she had worn at a ball in the days when she was courted by a young naval doctor who had been drowned at sea. Ring velvet, she said it was, of the finest quality, the sight of which upset her so much that she was glad to be rid of it. I spent the whole day closeted in my bedroom altering it to suit myself. Black showed up the fairness of my complexion and the gold of hair dressed in the Edwardian style. It would surely charm Mr Emerson. A white rose peeped from a low cut bodice; a voluminous skirt revealed just a suspicion of white stockinged ankles. I swept down the stairs determined to dazzle. The smile I had prepared to greet him who had been in my mind all day had to be wasted — on Jack O'Sullivan, a gay, young student from Trinity with a mop of dark curly hair. 'Begorrah,' he said, 'you're a sight for sore eyes, sweetheart.' Swirling me off my feet, he waltzed me across the hall and was just about to give me a smacking kiss on the lips when Mr Emerson, in a smart dinner jacket and a tray of glasses in his hand, intercepted us.

'Who's the swell?' enquired Jack. 'Your aunt's beau?'

A full moon, turned on like an arc light to flood the lawn and an old piano enticed couples to waltz. After a few drinks I was well away, but managed to keep my head. Determined that Jack should not ruin my evening I succeeded in evading him. While he was helping himself to whisky I sneaked out to Quarry Hill. At the wheezy creak of the gate in the back yard I leapt like a startled sheep, ripping my skirt on a bramble. The roof of The Peak gleamed like molten metal, the distant sea sparkled like mackerel. In the audible silence a throaty voice called me. Wading through bracken I ran into the arms of Mr Emerson. I searched his face. The moonlight aged him, made his iron grey hair as white as snow. Cupping my face in his hands, his eyes gazed at me with as mournful an intensity as had my grandmother's on the day I bid her farewell. Sharing his sadness, I leant my head on his shoulder. 'Your hair is damp,' he said, feeling it, exploring it. 'And your shoulder. You'll catch cold.' Taking off his dinner jacket he flung it over my shoulders, and solemnly, as though leading me to an altar, he led me to a boulder.

He asked, falteringly, almost apologetically, whether he was right in believing I was not indifferent to him. He couldn't expect me to marry him. Not yet; not until he had resigned from the Civil Service. He had the option of retiring on a pension and settling in Dublin in three years' time, or remaining indefinitely in India. What he did depended on me. He knew as soon as he first laid eyes on me at Kingstown Pier that I was the girl he had been waiting for all his life.

Had he waited in vain, he asked, tilting my face to his? Did he flatter himself that I cared for him?

Dare I confess that I didn't care for him as much as I cared that he should propose to me? His proposal was a credit in my account, a permanent flower for me to wear in place of the rose. I grasped the hand that had brushed a cobweb from my hair, and pressed it fervently to my lips. How he interpreted this I do not know. A cloud crossing the moon threw a shadow over the darkened hillside. Aunt Louisa called me loudly, shrilly. I leapt to my feet.

'For Heaven's sake,' I cried, pushing him back on the boulder from which he had risen to accompany me, 'stay where you are. My aunt will be furious if she sees us together.'

'I'm coming,' I called, striding through bracken as she came like a Fury to meet me.

Propelling me indoors by the scruff of the neck to her room, she banged the door and ordered me to give an account of myself. Who had pulled down my hair and ripped her dress from hem to waist? Was it Jack or Mr Emerson whom I had been spooning with on Quarry Hill? She wondered I hadn't more pride than to make myself cheap by throwing myself — she wouldn't say like what — at men. Had any of her patients or staff seen the sight I looked, I'd have brought disgrace on her and her house. The sooner she was quit of me the better. I was to go to my room and start packing. It would be many a long day before I would darken her door.

Stung, I presented her with a verbatim report of my suitor's tentative proposal. She snorted with surprise that Jim Emerson had made such a fool of himself. To propose marriage to a chit of a girl young enough to be his daughter. The poor man must have taken leave of his senses. Or else it was the drink talking. There was no telling what a man might say when he had a drop too much. I assured her he was perfectly sober.

'If you take him seriously,' she shouted, 'more fool you. I've had enough of your goings on. I saw the way you were behaving coming back in the gloaming from Glendalough. I'm not as blind as you'd like to believe. I had a good mind to send you packing there and then.'

The noise of a bolt being fastened in the back door silenced her. 'It's himself,' she cried in consternation. 'I don't want a scene. Quick. Off to bed.'

I had to obey. From the landing I heard Mr Emerson apologize for keeping me out so late without her permission. He owed her an explanation. Where was her niece?

'In bed, I hope,' she replied. 'Then may I have a word with you?' he politely enquired. She invited him into her room for a nightcap to take the chill out of his bones; and before the door closed on them I heard her say she had been obliged to scold me for disappearing from the party with the young O'Sullivan boy. I was never to know what further lies prevented him seeing me off in the morning. She had me up at dawn and out of the house before I saw Mr Emerson again.

'I don't blame Louisa,' said mother, when I told her the sad ending of my romance. 'For spoiling her last chance of making a good match you deserved what you got.'

7 Wimbledon

Our next move was from Wandsworth to a house at Wimbledon large enough to have a room for theosophical meetings on the ground floor. My father, further promoted in the Publicity Department at Westinghouse and with a further increase in salary, could afford to expand, to air his views in public, to pass on the message of the Mahatmas as it came to him through the work of Blavatsky.

He called the house White Lodge, after the Great White Lodge of the spiritual brotherhood of those who had the welfare of mankind at heart.

The Great White Lodge stood well back from a road encircling Wimbledon Hill, near the Common. Its front looked out on a shrubbery of evergreens. At the back was a wrought-iron balcony, draped by vines and wisteria which was a haze of mauve in spring. A grand piano imported by a wealthy American woman who had offered her services as my father's secretary occupied a place of honour under the picture of Master K. H. and enlarged photographs of Blavatsky and Besant.

To help her run an establishment which was now more like an institution than a home my mother had to rely on a daily char and the assistance of two of the more humble of my father's followers. One was the daughter of a country parson who offered her services in return for her keep. She had a room in the basement next to the large, gloomy kitchen. When little red-haired Elsie upset my mother she would squeak an apology, blush to the roots of her hair, and scuttle away to her dark hole under the stairs. She seemed to take pleasure in effacing herself. My brother alone brought animation to her watery blue eyes; if he condescended to tease her a sly smile crossed her freckled face.

She was inwardly happy it seemed because to have become a servant in my father's house made her a bit of a martyr and so furthered her spiritual evolution.

We had scarcely moved into our new home before every household in the land had heard that Britain had declared war.

Young men and women, and those who should have known better in villages, farms, stately homes, even mothers of sons of military age, were fired by a patriotic zeal which to my disgust and astonishment seemed to make them eager to sacrifice themselves and those dear to them for the sake of 'little Belgium'. From the beginning I was against it. Protected by my sex from having to participate in a war of which I disapproved I engaged in wordy warfare in defence of peace. I spoke with derision of the cheering crowds who awaited the appearance of King George and Queen Mary on the balcony of Buckingham Palace. Rather than rend the air with patriotic songs they should, in my opinion, have covered their heads in mourning for a catastrophe. Amongst my contemporaries only my brother shared my attitude. Instilled with Quaker principles at school, he openly declared himself a pacifist. War to him was organized mass murder. He would face a military tribunal as a conscientious objector rather than enlist. Whenever I passed a platoon of raw recruits marching through the streets on a cold winter morning sympathy for them made me not only rage against those who had the power to send them away but made me feel personally guilty for not being involved. The cheerful innocence I thought I perceived on the faces of many of those not much older than myself was a reproach to my militant smugness.

The war crushed the hopes my father had cherished of establishing a flourishing theosophical centre at White Lodge. He had to content himself with an audience of elderly women with private means who busied themselves while listening to him in helping the war effort by knitting comforters and socks for the troops. There was a sprinkling of men too old for military service. I considered theosophists people remote from me and I seldom attended the weekend meetings.

Then I found that for which I had been almost consciously searching. Or rather, he found me. He fell in love with me at first sight — so he said. It was little Elsie who seemed to be the instrument of destiny.

Her hand tapped at my bedroom door one warm June evening.

I had forgotten the German invasion of France in reading of the French invasion of Russia in Tolstoy's *War and Peace*.

My father had asked her to find out whether I was at home. Did I know it was White Lotus Day? I said what had that got to do with me. She knew the meetings bored me. But this was to be a special occasion. Mrs Leisingring, my father's secretary, had invited a couple of musicians from the Royal College to play before and after the lecture. It might do me good, cheer me up, make me forget myself, if I came to the meeting, just for once, to please my father.

Much against my inclination I said I would. I didn't know that the violinist would be standing with a fiddle tucked under his chin waiting for me to creep into the back of the meeting room. I noticed that he nudged the pianist and whispered something in his ear that made him smile and turn his head in my direction. I presumed he was calling his attention to Cliff Thomson, buttoned into the uniform of the Officers' Training Corps, who had stood up to beckon me to a vacant seat next to his in the back row. Gibson couldn't know that Cliff, although ostensibly my brother's friend more than mine, had a crush on me. The faces of my father and his secretary were in shadow. Was my mother, seated in the front row, knitting, listening to the music or to the telepathic communication that I felt there was between my father and the American lady? A dying chord vibrated into silence. My father rose to deliver his address. I seemed to know a lot of it already.

'Man,' he said, 'is obliged to share his intrinsic isolation with the rest of mankind. We in this room this evening not only share with one another the peril that threatens our island, but share the adventure of exploring the uncharted seas which lie beyond the charted shores of our circumscribed human personalities. Even as Columbus had faith in the existence of America before he set out on his voyage, so must we have faith in the existence of a spiritual world before we can venture to explore its manifestations. Let us take heart. In this dark age — the *kali-uga* of Hindu scriptures — H. P. Blavatsky has provided us with a chart to aid our exploration of the virgin lands that lay about us in our infancy and to which we, as man, intrinsically belong. Evolution is a spiritual process; a process by which we have evolved from our simian ancestors to the stature of man. And man today is but an infant in comparison to that which he will eventually become. Becoming is the essence of man. It is this essence I speak of when I speak of spirit.'

Cliff nudged me. 'The violinist,' he muttered, 'has been trying to give you the glad eye ever since your old man started letting off steam.'

He was standing with his back to the window. I raised myself in the chair the better to see him, and was struck by the delicacy of his hand, by his long ashblond hair swept back from a domed forehead to the nape of his neck. My father had finished. He smiled, nodded slightly and, cradling his fiddle as affectionately as if it were a girl, at a nod from the pianist he struck the strings with his bow.

As a round of applause greeted the close of a sonata which I afterwards learnt was by César Franck, Cliff hauled me to my feet. A cigarette at his lips he edged me through members of the audience who were making for the door and out into the hall to the front steps. The smell of a syringa bush in flower at the gate mixed with that of tar and dust. I agreed that we should go for a stroll on the Common.

We had reached the brow of the hill when who should we see cycling rapidly towards us, his hat on the handlebar, wind ruffling his hair, but the violinist.

'Well, I'll be damned!' exploded Cliff.

'Excuse me butting in,' said my pursuer, drawing up neatly beside us. 'You are Miss Dunlop?' I asked how he knew.

He had pointed me out to a little red-haired woman with glasses as I was making a dash for the door. She had not only established my identity but provided him with a clue as to where I had gone. His friend Eric, the pianist, had lent him his cycle. 'You see,' he said, grinning, 'where there's a will there's a way. I've tracked you down.'

I was both put off by his self-assurance and flattered that he had come chasing after me. As he sat poised on the saddle, one foot on a pedal, I noticed the leanness of his shoulder blades and a bony knee. There was a faint tan on his aquiline features but I could not tell the colour of his heavily lidded eyes. He introduced himself. He was Gibson Young, an Australian who had come to study the violin under Dr Brodsky at Manchester, and who was at present taking a teachers' training course at the Royal College of Music. I introduced Cliff, whom he had hitherto ignored, as my brother's friend. Cliff nodded curtly, lit a cigarette, and enquired,

I.O.—E

not without malice, whether being an Aussie had exempted him from military service.

'Your climate is to blame,' he said.

He had twice tried to enlist, but had been turned down as physically unfit for the Army by the doctors who had traced his attacks of asthma to a patch on one lung caused by pneumonia during his first winter in Manchester.

He looked surprised when I congratulated him on his lucky escape.

'Well,' he said, briskly, 'now that I have done what I wanted I must push off. Eric will be livid. He's waiting at the station with my fiddle. We're sharing digs.'

He shook hands with Cliff, wished him all the best, and mounting with a gay 'I'll be seeing you, Miss Dunlop', free-wheeled off down the hill.

'Is that a threat,' growled Cliff, 'or a promise?'

What happened to me was what I wanted to happen. I wanted to be forced into a new existence. Gibson came to the house at weekends, scattering gifts as lavishly as though money was no object. Considering his health, his vitality was extraordinary; it affected everyone within reach. Unlike most artistic Australians I have met since, he was not shy. I suspected right way, and I came to know I was right, that his surface buoyancy masked a deeper melancholy; it was his distrust of himself that made him so cocksure.

Although my mother objected in theory to his extravagance and criticized him for it, she raised no objection to his adding wine and the delicacies so hard to come by in wartime to our evening meal. He named Elsie his Marmalade Cat, complimented her on her vegetarian cooking, and stroked her ruddy hair. He encouraged my brother to discuss art, teased him about the girl students at the art classes he attended in the evening, admired his work. For my father he had a respect amounting to deference. He tactfully listened to his opinions and refrained from expressing his own: consequently, within a month or so of our first meeting, he was accepted almost as a member of the household, and as my 'intended'. Of all the possible suitors whom in day-dreams I had imagined coming to seek my hand, Gibson of the hooded eyes, blond hair, pallid skin and sensitive hands was the least expected. I had not yet learnt that it is the unexpected which usually happens.

His admiration gave me a newly found confidence in myself. But I could not seriously think of him as a lover. A lover would have taken me by storm, and he hadn't. My head filled with such notions, I evaded him. But it was different when I watched him from a distant corner of the sitting-room whilst he was playing. His fingers on the strings became vibrant with a separate life of their own. I fell in love with his fingers. Once he had concentrated on the score, too dedicated to the music to be aware of me, he became necessary to me. I wanted him. Yet when he first pro- posed to me, I laughed.

'You've been drinking,' I taunted, as though I had been Aunt Louisa. 'Your so-called love for me is an alcoholic aberration.'

'If you're not the limit,' he cried, rolling his eyes in despair. 'I tell a girl I love her, ask her to be my wife, and she has the cheek to accuse me of being the worse for drink. I'll make you pay for this, you outrageous little flirt.'

He paid me out by failing to turn up the following weekend to take me for an outing in town as he had promised. Trying in vain to hide my disappointment from mother's observant eye, I hung about waiting for him. Mother sat inspecting me at supper as though she were a member of a jury and I a prisoner. She stung me out of my silence by saying that she strongly disapproved of Gibson's behaviour.

'What behaviour?' I asked, glowering at her. Her eyes were as bright as an inquisitive child's, her cheeks pink. The deliberate way she poured herself out another cup of tea warned me she was getting ready to strike me a blow.

Did I know that Gibson was engaged to a girl in Australia before he left home? If I didn't, it was disgraceful of him to have deceived me. I let the information she flung at me sink down into me; it echoed sharply and then subsided, leaving scarcely a ripple in my mind. I retaliated by telling her that as Gibson had proposed to me last Saturday and I had refused him, his engage- ment, whether true or false, was no concern of mine.

'You refused him?' she repeated as though she couldn't believe it. 'So that's why he hasn't turned up!'

Without waiting for any further revelations from her, I ran out of the kitchen, slammed the door after me, and dashed out of the house to the Common. My fury against Gibson for keeping his engagement a secret was matched by the fury with which an east wind lashed the trees. Thank heavens I had the sense to treat his premature proposal in the way it deserved. If he ever came chasing after me again, I'd give him hell. But suppose he had taken seriously what I intended only as a snub and failed to turn up again. I'd be left high and dry to hug my resentment to myself. I was wounded where I was most vulnerable — in my feminine pride. Was it the pain of an old, half-forgotten wound inflicted by an imagined rejection in childhood that seemed to pull at my heart?

He did come back. The tenderness of his hand stroking hair from my eyes told me that he had in truth broken off his engagement to be free to marry me. It had been a ghastly mistake to pledge himself to a girl older than himself for whom he felt gratitude and respect rather than love. I believe he had told my mother to spite me for hurting him. My confidence restored, I was prepared to be generous. I agreed to marry him once he was earning enough to support me. Wedged between his thighs I returned his kisses with an ardour equal to his own. I trusted him. His tongue probing my ear gave me a physical pleasure equal to Mr Emerson's fondling my breast.

After he'd gone a restlessness that made sleep impossible drove me from my bed. I crept downstairs in my nightgown past my parents' room to the kitchen to get a drink of water. My mother heard me. She called me to come in; she wanted to speak to me.

As always when waiting for my father's return from one of those many engagements that kept him out to well after midnight she was propped up in bed, reading by the light of her bedside lamp. She still looked handsome. Regarding me over her glasses, she beckoned me to sit beside her on the bed. I waited for the scolding.

To my surprise she began to praise Gibson to me. She enumerated his qualities like an auctioneer. She admired his spontaneous warmth, his unfailing good humour and, although recklessly extravagant considering he was still dependent on his father, to be generous was better than to be mean. She understood he wanted to marry when he could afford to keep me. As I would not be likely to get another offer in a hurry, would it not be right to accept him?

'You advise me to become engaged?' I asked tentatively.

'I advise you to make up your mind what you intend to do.'

'Suppose I don't know? Suppose I'm too young to know for certain what I feel for Gibson.'

'You have nothing to recommend you but your youth,' she said with a harshness that still stings. 'I think it would not only be rash but foolish to refuse him.'

I stared at her as though unable to believe my ears. It seemed incredible that she could think so little of her daughter. I jumped up from the bed with a harsh laugh and had reached the door when she called me back.

'Won't you kiss me goodnight?' she said with an odd sort of wistfulness. 'I didn't mean to hurt you. In the war there are so few eligible young men to pick and choose from that I was only thinking of your future. I want you to be happy.'

I gave her a hasty peck on her cheek and promised to act on her advice.

I believed Gibson knew the answers to all the questions about sex of which I was so ignorant. I should learn them by sleeping with him when the opportunity came. The war dragged on. The prospect of marriage was distant.

I was hurt that my father seemed to take little interest in my engagement other than to admire the ring Gibson had given me. He merely warned me that to be married in haste was to repent at leisure. He said that since the end of the war was not yet in sight I had time to repent before the wedding.

To spite my mother for her readiness to palm me off, I agreed to allow Gibson to sleep with me — under her very nose so to speak. Spring was in the air. Green incense wreathed from the bole of an elm at the end of the garden. I lay in bed waiting, as we'd arranged, until my brother was asleep, so that Gibson could sneak unobserved across the landing from his room to mine.

I turned my back to the door as I heard the handle turned; lay rigid, with eyes closed, pretending to be asleep. Gibson flung off his pyjamas and slipped into bed. A cold foot grazed my leg. I hadn't expected the smoothness of his naked body; nor that he would raise knees to make a lap for me to lie on.

'Your skin smells of chrysanthemums,' he whispered, kissing a pulse on my neck. Had he broken the spell, or had his hand on my groin sounded an alarm signal? Without warning, I leapt from the bed. After me in an instant, he gathered me in his arms. Grasping a dishevelled lock of hair I tugged it, laughed in his face, as he bore me to the dressing-table mirror.

'Look at yourself,' he ordered. 'See how sweet you are.' The mirror reflected our entwined bodies. I lay across his chest, an arm dangling to his thigh, a face upraised from falling hair. His shoulders looked ivory. I giggled, as bending to kiss me, his hair tickled my cheek.

'You see,' he said, stifling a cough, 'that we are right together, that we belong.'

'I can hear your heart beat,' I said.

'You hear the pump. My heart I have given away to a heartless woman who could twist me round her little finger.'

'It's true,' I responded. 'I am heartless. I don't know how to love.'

'Then it's up to me to teach you.'

Ignoring my protest he hauled me back to bed. Kisses light as petals fell gently on face, on eyes, on breast. He made a pillow of his arm. A wave carried me away and I lay stranded beneath his weight. His tongue opened my lips.

'Don't move,' he said, and I did not dare to.

I shared the phantasy common, I believe, to many a young girl at the time that babies came from the navel. The risk of pregnancy never entered my head. My first night with Gibson made me hungry for more sex; and I would have been perfectly willing to repeat it since he had assured me that I could trust him to take every precaution against discovery and I believed him — had I not been prevented by a totally unfounded conviction that there was something physically wrong with me. I felt maimed, unfit for marriage, unable to bear a child. This neurotic anxiety complicated my already complicated feelings for Gibson: made me liable to sporadic fits of temper. Obsessed with myself and my emotional problems, I could not concentrate on my work at the Teachers' Training College; consequently I failed dismally at the end-of-term examinations. Feeling doubly a failure, my anxiety left me no peace.

I decided that were I unable to have children, then I would not marry at all. But before taking the drastic step of breaking off my engagement, I should make certain; I should be examined by a doctor. I made an appointment with our family doctor, an elderly, paternal, kindly man, who had attended me when I had produced all the symptoms of scarlet fever after having been in contact with a girl who had it at school. He attributed my symptoms to hypersensitivity; I could trust him to be sympathetic. As an excuse for seeking a consultation I complained of severe menstrual pains. The fee I took for him was two guineas that Gibson had given me to buy accessories for a suit he was having made for me by his tailor.

I was a sheep and the doctor the shearer. I lay rigid on the couch, my hands clenched against a convulsive twitching, my eyes fixed on a stain on the ceiling. The ordeal over, I waited for his verdict. He could see nothing wrong with me apart from a slight congestion of the uterus. I should keep my bowels open before the period fell due.

'I noticed,' he said, twiddling his fountain pen, 'that you are wearing a ring on your engagement finger. Are you engaged to be married?'

I was? Then he must put a delicate question to me. Had I had connection with my fiancé? I returned a blank stare. 'Have you slept with him?' he asked testily. I was obliged to confess that I once had.

'Ah,' he reflected with relief, 'that explains your anxiety. If you want to know whether you are in the family way, I can set your mind at rest. Your young man must have taken adequate precautions to prevent pregnancy. Luckily no harm has yet been done. You took a grave risk, mind you: a risk that I advise you not to repeat unless you want to bring trouble on yourself and your family. Don't be foolish enough to conceive a child out of wedlock. It's a bad beginning to a marriage.'

He leant across the desk to lay a friendly hand on mine. 'Take the advice of an old man,' he said with a kindly twinkle in his shrewd grey eyes, 'and keep that young man of yours waiting until after the marriage register is signed. Once you're married you may have as many children as your means allow. If necessary, you may count on me to attend your first confinement.'

I had learnt what I wanted to know. If there had been anything wrong with me he would have found out. Thanking him effusively, I offered him the fee.

Since our engagement Gibson had become a sort of parent. He gave me pocket money and paid for my clothes.

Having seen me act heroine in Masefield's *Tragedy of Man* at a performance given by the students of the College at the end of the Christmas term he became convinced that I had acting talent and we tried to persuade my parents to let me train for the stage. My mother told him not to fill my head with nonsense; my father, that a stage career would interfere with marriage. He listened to neither. If they refused to pay, he would. He arranged an audition for me with the Principal of the Royal Albert Hall Dramatic School. The course was in elocution, dramatic literature and play production.

Hobble skirts were the vogue. I was a Gibson Girl. The suit he had ordered for me made from fine Scotch tweed fitted perfectly. A little jacket fluted out over a sheaf of skirt that had a slit up the side to show my leg. Worn with a felt hat that had a narrow turned-up brim and a white shirt blouse, all I needed was a riding crop. When my mother saw her dowdy daughter so transformed she remarked acidly that it would take a small fortune to live up to that rig-out.

I lived up to it at the audition with the Principal of the Drama School. I wanted to do Gibson justice. Miss Elsie Fogarty did me the honour to say that I bore a strong resemblance to Ellen Terry in her youth; the set of the eyes was strikingly similar, and I had a similar tragic frown. (I presume she referred to the line between my brows — a stigma due to astigmatism — which I bear to this day).

'See what you can make of this,' she said, handing me the potion scene from *Romeo and Juliet*. It was just right for me. I knew it by heart, and therefore could deliver it with a passionate intensity which I was sure deserved the praise it earned. She was less enthusiastic about what I made of a scene from *The Rivals*. An actress must be versatile. I would need to develop a feeling for comedy. Otherwise I would stand little chance of getting a part either in a touring company or in repertory.

She told me she thought I had talent. If I worked hard at voice production, mime and deportment, she saw no reason why I should not have a stage career.

To please Gibson and to justify his faith in me, I worked conscientiously in a group of girls whose vanity exceeded their intelligence. Their superior sophistication, their clothes, their knowledge of make-up, made me feel outwardly inferior, inwardly superior.

The pleasure my fellow students got from self-display showed me how exhibitionist they were. As for me, I realized I was far too much the egotist to enjoy being other than myself.

I saw I was a fraud. I cheated Gibson into believing I wanted to become an actress, when really I only wanted to be a wife and mother. After that I would — perhaps — take up acting seriously. At the Dramatic School I was marking time. But I gained a certificate for teaching drama, voice production, stage technique, a piece of embossed parchment with my name enscrolled in gothic type which I gave to Gibson to keep, a bill of credit for our joint account which might come in useful some day.

I awoke one morning feeling feverish and sick. I vomited so prodigiously that I went back to bed. Mother, dressed in her best, ready to leave with Elsie for a Conference of the Star in the East, at which Krishna Murti and Annie Besant were to preside, appeared at the door to ask what was wrong. She thought it was one of my periodic gastric attacks. There was nothing to be done but to stay in bed and eat nothing until I felt better. She would send Elsie up with a jug of water, and off she went to the Conference.

I dozed, perspiring, until I was woken into a green and sunny world by a cool hand on my forehead. It was Gibson's. I smiled. He fussed. I was running a temperature? Where would he find a thermometer? Why had everyone disappeared? He cursed them for leaving me ill in bed in a deserted house. He'd tell my mother what he thought of her. I believe Gibson saved my life.

He insisted on fetching a doctor against my mother's wishes. She didn't see the sense in calling in a doctor for a bilious attack. I was accustomed to gastric trouble. Contemptuously demanding Dr Ferguson's address, he shot out of the room. The high fever detached me from my body and I felt at peace. The doctor came in followed by my mother and Gibson. He took my temperature, sounded my chest, and then ordered the others to leave the room. The examination over, he settled me comfortably on the pillows, pulled up the bedclothes, and telling me with a playful pat on the cheek that I was a brave lass, went briskly from the room. I watched a moth circling around the light bulb. I traced with a hand arcs in the air, broken arcs, like everything so far in my life. Nothing I had attempted had been completed, nothing brought to a conclusion. Death would complete the broken arc. I did not fear death then.

The anxiety in Gibson's face as he knelt by the bed, told me that something serious was wrong. I ran a hot hand through his hair; and he explained haltingly that I was suffering from an acute inflammation of the appendix. To avoid the danger of peritonitis, Dr Ferguson had insisted on an immediate operation.

He had telephoned a surgeon and arranged with the local hospital for a bed. An ambulance should arrive within an hour.

I had a sacrificial smile as the orderlies wrapped me like a mummy in a scarlet blanket and hoisted me gently from the bed to a stretcher. Like bakers shove a loaf into an oven, they slipped me on to a bunk in the white interior of the ambulance. Gibson climbed in. The door closed on my mother's tearful promise to turn up later at the hospital. I felt delirious. I was off in a sleigh with a ringing bell.

As soon as a door opened noiselessly to receive the trolley that was bearing me away from Gibson my mood changed. I felt trapped, doomed to obey commands, forced to have a mask clamped over my face, obliged to bear its suffocating sickliness, to breathe deeply, to count aloud. Terrified that my voice would fail before I was unconscious and that I would still feel, I shouted soundlessly. A hand that clutched at air refused to move. I was being sucked through a dark tunnel towards a white light.

No sky had ever seemed so blue, no June so green, as that which my eyes beheld the day I left the hospital. A mother temporarily chastened reserved her censure for my father. He was never there in a crisis. He had been at home neither whilst I was in hospital, nor when my brother had faced the conscientious objectors' tribunal. As an alternative to prison Ronald had been offered work in a munition factory or on the land. He had decided on a farm and was waiting for a place to go.

Dr Ferguson insisted so much that my mother agreed I should go for a couple of weeks to the seaside. I don't know why she chose Herne Bay. Perhaps she thought it would be cheap. If, as I believe, it was to save themselves trouble that my parents allowed me to go alone with Gibson, they could not complain we made the most of an unofficial honeymoon. Nothing could have been less hospitable than the dingy boarding house in a back street in which Gibson, deceived by an advertisement, had booked two rooms. A thunderstorm, and the deposit, made us give it a trial for a couple of days. It was arranged that the convalescent should breakfast in bed.

'You two might as well muck in together,' said the landlady as she plonked a breakfast tray for two on the table. It was her way of saying that she had already seen Gibson leaving my room in his dressing gown. 'Saves me the trouble of laying the table. Alright?'

'Fine,' we agreed. We spent the best part of the morning in bed. Gibson was a good lover. He knew when to sweep aside resistance and how to prolong pleasure by using self control. He was all tenderness. To Gibson my breasts were identical twins to whom he gave each a name and upon whom it was his duty to lavish an equal attention. Enticed by the bold but featherlight stroke of fingers uncurling in secret places, I threw all caution away.

8 Manchester

I kept my morning sickness to myself and forced myself to eat breakfast. I couldn't be going to have a baby. It must be an aftermath of the appendicitis. I imagined that if I'd conceived I should have known it for sure. But Gibson, on hearing I had missed two successive periods, insisted on taking me to his doctor who said I was pregnant.

Gibson said he didn't mind at all that he would have to bear the responsibility of a wife and child even if he didn't have any money. We would simply be married sooner than we had intended.

'It's the best day's work I ever did,' he said jubilantly. To celebrate it, we'd be married in a church and not in some pokey registry office. I didn't mind either because at last my wish to bear a child was to be fulfilled.

The thought of having to break the news to my parents, especially to my father, whom he expected to be angry, brought on an attack of his asthma. Seeing him lean, gasping, on the gate I suggested we should postpone telling them until after we were married. He wouldn't hear of it.

My mother might be furious at first, but she'd probably be relieved that a hasty marriage would spare her the expense of providing me with a trousseau. Would I find out when it would be convenient for my father to see him? In the meantime he would put up the banns at the local Congregational Church, to which his parents belonged in Australia, and start looking for a job in an orchestra.

My father spoke to me rather than I to him. With a twinkle in his eye he flung an arm round my shoulder, and tilting my chin, searched my eyes. Was he right in believing I was expecting a baby?

I hid my face on his shoulder. 'Now, now,' he encouraged, patting my head. 'There's nothing to be ashamed of. Such things happen in the best of well-regulated families.'

'But how did you guess, Father? Is it so obvious?' I anxiously enquired. 'Does Mother know?'

An old married man like himself should know from experience how a woman looks when she's in the family way. He hadn't thought it wise to mention it to mother until he was sure. How many months was I gone?

Three? Then it was high time I did something about it. When did we intend to be married?

He seemed relieved to hear that it was within a couple of weeks, but said he was doubtful whether Gibson could earn enough as a musician to support a wife, at any rate until after the war. He would see what he could find for him at Westinghouse.

I was deeply moved when he gave me a warm and lingering kiss on the lips.

There weren't any jobs in orchestras. Gibson had to take a job on the clerical staff of the Westinghouse Munition Works at Old Trafford, Manchester. He gave up his further training for my sake.

There was a fog on our wedding day. Of the conflicting feelings I had as I said farewell to the bedroom at the top of the house, two predominated: gratitude for the treasure under my belly and fear that what had been conceived out of wedlock might (as Dr Ferguson had warned) be an obstacle to a happy marriage. As a prospective mother I felt blessed; as a bride-to-be a homeless waif with nothing but a suitcase of old clothes and a black astrakhan coat, the worse for wear, bequeathed from her mother's wardrobe.

Gibson was determined to honour his wedding day. He turned up at the local Congregational church in pinstriped trousers, tail coat, a topper, and with a white carnation in his buttonhole. Flinging open the door of the hired Daimler, he presented me with a posy of violets and lily-of-the-valley, my mother with a bunch of white chrysanthemums. As my mother followed us up the steps to the church, I heard her remark acidly to my father that Gibson should count his pennies instead of playing the grandee.

'Let the poor fellow have his fling — this day of all days,' said father.

A verger conducted us into a bleak, ill-lit vestry to await the arrival of the minister; and while Gibson went off to look for Eric Masters who had promised to act as best man my father took me aside to a window blanketed in fog.

'Gibson,' he began, laying a hand on my shoulder, 'is not the husband I would have chosen for you, had I the choice. But his readiness to accept his responsibility is all to the good, and since I believe that you met and were attracted to one another in accordance with the *Karma,* I daresay it will work out all right.'

He likewise believed that the *being* of the child I was to have had chosen me as the vehicle through which to incarnate into the world. All a parent could do was to provide according to his means and ability the best environment he could for the development of his children whilst allowing each the freedom to follow his own particular destiny. I may not have approved of the environment he and mother had given me, but at least I could not accuse them of having unduly interfered with my freedom.

'I have faith,' he said gravely, 'in my daughter. I know her to be capable of taking the consequences of her actions with courage.'

I was near to tears when the verger tapped him on the shoulder. 'Beg pardon, sir,' he said, 'I thought I should remind you to have the ring handy.'

'Me have the ring handy? You have made a mistake,' said my father, twinkling at him quizzically. 'I'm the bride's father. I am here to give her away.'

Mother cut short the old man's apologies by assuring him that to be considered young enough to be the bridegroom was a compliment her husband was not likely to forget in a hurry.

Feeling deserted by a father who could so levelheadedly give me into another man's keeping, I promised to love and honour, though not to obey (since Gibson had that injunction omitted from the ceremony) Ernest Gibson Young.

As the Wedding March swelled out in the empty church Gibson led his unblushing bride past the long rows of pews as proudly as though he faced a packed congregation.

'A wedding,' sniffed mother, dabbing her eyes, 'is almost as solemn an occasion as a funeral. I nearly broke down.'

'Gibson,' she whispered, offering me a cheek for a kiss, 'has done all in his power to make amends. Do your best to make him a good wife.'

I promised I would try.

After a wedding night spent in a dismal station hotel in Manchester, Gibson left me to myself whilst he combed the district near the Munition Works for accommodation suitable for his bride. All he could find were two dingy back rooms packed with furniture in a quasi-respectable street near Old Trafford which the landlady condescended to offer for thirty shillings a week.

Despite my effort to act the part of a respectable married woman, Mrs Jones's sharp eyes soon detected my condition. On the pretext that I had dried my husband's socks and my 'smalls' at her sitting-room fire without her permission she gave me a week's notice. The steam was already loosening the wallpaper. I should send my dirty clothes to the laundry.

'I can't afford to send underclothing to the laundry.'

'And I can't afford to have you save money at my expense. A week come next Saturday you're to quit my house. Understand?' she shouted at me.

I lost my temper. I told her she was a nasty, spiteful old woman, and the sooner I saw the last of her the better.

She returned the compliment. I was a nasty, sly bit of goods, and she reckoned my husband had put up the banns just in time. It was easy to see I was in the family way. She wasn't going to have no expectant mothers in her house. I could get out quick and sharp.

'If you don't,' she threatened, as she shuffled from the room, 'I shall call the police and have you chucked out.'

I was spurred into action. I went immediately to the Public Library and looked through the local paper for advertisements, and was lucky enough to be able to get out before the specified time.

The two rooms on the ground floor of a neat little villa, set back from a tree-lined avenue in the respectable suburb of Hale, on the border of Cheshire, seemed positively luxurious.

Gibson and I could hardly believe it as we sat drinking tea in a comfortable, spotlessly clean front room looking out on a tidy garden which had rose bushes marching to the door.

'Takes a woman to find the right place,' said Gibson, grinning at me with satisfaction. 'I don't know how you've done it, Mimi darling.' Since he had become conscious of my swelling belly when making love, I was Mimi.

'Don't count your chickens before they're hatched.'

'It sounds as though you're expecting twins.'

'Hush,' I said, rising to close the door that our landlady had left ajar. 'Mrs Rogers is no more to be trusted than old Ma Jones.'

I was right. Mrs Rogers had no more compunction than her predecessor in getting rid of us. On the excuse of needing our rooms for relatives from Birmingham she politely asked me to leave at the end of the month. At least it was a month's notice instead of a week's.

After wandering about aimlessly looking for the best part of a day, I came upon an unpaved, rutted road leading to a gate facing open country. I leant against the gate and watched the birds. Green winter grain sprinkled ploughed fields rising to a belt of bare trees between me and the skyline.

If birds could find a home for their young, why not I? I clasped my hands and prayed as earnestly as I had at my grand-mother's knee to her bountiful God to aid me in finding a home fit for my child. Thrilled by a blackbird's song, I kept a sharp look-out as I retraced my steps down the rough road; and sure enough, on a road running parallel I saw a *To Let* board on the gate of a new brick two-storied house.

A waddling run brought me to a patch of grass in the front garden. Blank windows reflected the sunset. Believing that a house too large for my needs had been given to me in answer to my prayer I memorized the name and address of the agent on the signboard and went straight to Carter and Hollis, estate agents and auctioneers, and presented myself with as much dignity as I could to an elderly, spectacled man seated behind an enormous desk. Necessity spurred me to eloquence. As references I gave him my husband's office address and that of his London bank. Perhaps though it was mother's astrakhan coat that induced him to promise that, pending the receipt of twenty-five pounds in pay-ment of the first quarter's rent in advance, he would give me an option on the property. Without a penny to my name, but happy in the possession of keys to view Number Eight Woodford Avenue, I left the office convinced that the house was mine.

On Lady Day, precisely when the rent fell due, it was another miracle for Gibson to get a cheque for fifty pounds as a belated wedding present from his parents. After the rent was paid it would leave nearly twenty pounds with which to furnish the house. I bought a bed, a second-hand gate-leg table and settee for the back parlour. Otherwise we made do with oddments from junk shops and orange boxes. I scrubbed my gratitude to a God and a beneficent father-in-law into the floor boards and made cretonne curtains to cover the bay windows. Golden dandelions studded the tangled grass of the back garden. I rejoiced to feel the baby leap about in my womb like a salmon.

Gibson never complained about the coughing that kept him awake at night. Bowed like an old man he had to sit on the bed struggling for breath before he could leave for work in the morning. His sole complaint was about my increasing frigidity. Since my belly had become a drum I didn't want him to make love to me. Instead of responding as I had previously on a Sunday morning I drew apart to the edge of the bed or lay like a log in his arms.

'Give yourself to me, as you used to before you were pregnant,' he would demand. 'I'm not going to hurt you or the child. Love alone makes poverty tolerable. You are more interested in a cloud crossing the sky, the flight of a bird or sunlight streaking a wall than you are in me. It seems that all you wanted from me was a child. And now that you're satisfied, I'm not needed any more.'

I pleaded with him to be patient. It was in vain. Sometimes I would return his embrace with a simulated ardour that failed to deceive him. Sometimes he would fling himself from the bed in a rage, and bewailing his fate in marrying a frigid woman leave me in tears.

One day I lifted a corner of the curtain on the bay window and saw a lanky young man in a bulky oilskin with a weathered old hat pulled over his eyes who came tramping in mud-caked gumboots up the garden path. It was my brother! My mother had given him my address, and as he had a free half day at the farm, he thought he'd look me up. Over a tea of bread and marge in the back parlour we behaved as politely as though we had just been introduced for the first time. Stroking his beard with a workhardened hand, nails encrusted with clay, he droned on about his life at a Cheshire farm without a thought for me. It reminded me of home all over again. He had had a hard winter. Up before dawn, he had to trudge through seas of mud to a shed to milk cows by the light of a hurricane lamp. Out in all weathers lifting and carting beet, he now had the easier job of hoeing fields of cabbage and beans. 'The scent of bean fields in flower', his eyes lighting up in a smile, 'is a treat at this time of the year.'

Hearing about his life I forgot my own. I heard the farmer shout: 'Conchy, you blockhead, get a move on. What do ye think

I.O.—F

you're bloody well here for? A rest cure?' Or the cowman, a rheumaticky old man with whom he shared an attic at the farm, snigger at him for not knowing how to handle a tit at his age. 'Grip the bloody udder,' he ordered. 'Don't fiddle about with it.' The tractor driver was his chief enemy. A burly, good-looking fellow, he thought conscientious objectors were scum, traitors to King and country who should be made to face a firing squad, or to stop bullets in the front line. Ronald knew him to be spoiling for a fight and kept his distance; on the one occasion when he had made bold to ask the fellow what had stopped *him* from stopping bullets, he received a punch in the jaw that knocked him out flat.

The only alternative to them were a couple of fellow COs. Let out on parole from a local prison they had previously been serving sentences of solitary confinement for the duration of the war, he had met them once or twice at a club run by the vicar at the church hall on Saturday evenings. Queer chaps, fanatically sincere, they seemed to take a positive pleasure in suffering for their convictions, and because he didn't they treated him with a condescension that made him almost as uncomfortable as the scorn of the tractor driver.

He startled me by casually announcing that he intended to get married as soon as he was quit of the farm.

'Married at your age!' I cried in protest. 'You haven't even begun to earn a living. How can you possibly support a wife?'

'I'm relying on Flora to help me out,' he said, grinning in his beard. 'Flora's my girl. She's no beauty by ordinary standards — a bit on the heavy side: more like a Flemish madonna than Botticelli's goddess. But she's the most heavenly blue eyes I've ever seen, and hair that she can sit on, black and glossy as a raven.'

He had met her when out sketching and had shown her his roughs of barns, horse ploughs, groups of trees, anything he thought might come in useful for landscapes later on. She admired them. They started talking as though they had known each other all their lives.

'She loves me,' he continued rapturously. 'Loves a hobbledehoy like me, and has faith in me. She believes I shall make my name as a painter.'

'The point is,' I said, 'do you love her?'

'She is the other half of myself,' he replied with such conviction that I envied him.

'Older than you?'

'Yes. But that's all to the good. Her old man's a wealthy Lancashire industrialist and he can afford to give her an allowance. And she is determined to see that he does. She is ready to support me until I can get a start. I'll bring her along to see you one day. I'm sure you'll like Flora. Humour's not her strong point, but insight is. She can see through a person to what he actually is.'

'You'd better wait until after my confinement. You're so wrapped up in your own affairs that you don't seem to have noticed my condition.'

'Couldn't miss it if I tried,' he returned twinkling.

'Then why didn't you mention it?'

'Thought it might be a delicate subject,' he admitted shyly.

'When's it due?'

'Should be at the end of next month.'

'Not long to wait now,' and he put a hand on my shoulder. Wishing me the best of luck, he said that unless he pushed off at once he'd keep Flora waiting. He had arranged to meet her in Manchester on his way back to the farm.

The evening before the pains began, believing my time was near, I took my cumbersome body upstairs to the bedroom and, lighting a candle in the gathering darkness, lowered my weight carefully on to the bed. Presently I closed my eyes as though in prayer that all might be well, and I felt a hand slip gently to the nape of my neck, just under my hair, and clasp it tenderly, protectively, as though to give me courage to face my ordeal. Believing Gibson had returned earlier than usual, I turned round expecting to find him standing behind me. Nobody was there. It was uncanny to feel the handclasp and yet to be alone in the shadowy room! A great sense of well-being welled up within me. All fear of my coming ordeal vanished in the presence of what I am credulous enough to believe was the spirit of my unborn child. Oddly enough, my son, both in his boyhood and as a man, has a habit of clasping my neck tenderly to console me should I be distressed. That evening I knew, with a certainty my husband called wish fulfilment, that I was to have a son, a son whom I felt would be a clearer, stronger, more loving character than myself. I decided, there and then, to call him Michael.

The sole connection between my angelic visitor and the sleeping infant, wrapped in a shawl, whom the gnome-like midwife placed in my arms after I woke from a drugged sleep was the name. I thought his flushed cheeks and downy head perfect.

Tracing a likeness to my father in his mouth and chin, it was as though my father had returned in the shape of a son. My husband, haggard and hollow-eyed from lack of sleep, approached the bed almost humbly.

'You've had an awful time, darling,' he said, embracing us both. 'Twenty-seven hours of labour.'

Parting the shawl so that he could admire his son, I assured him it had been worth it; and as Michael's fist closed on his thumb he seemed to agree.

I don't know for how many days after that first reunion I hovered in fever on a borderland between fantasy and reality. Obliged to leave Michael to the midwife, I was in a limbo in which consciousness ebbed and flowed.

I woke one evening, bathed in sweat, yet unaccountably and deliciously cool, as though I had been washed by a dark tide to a sunny shore. The whitewashed walls of the bedroom were flooded by the gold of sunset.

From a diagram of male figures doing various exercises which Gibson had hung from a gasbracket, to remind him to do the same, my eyes wandered to a woman seated in a rocking chair with her back to me, nursing a white bundle in a shawl. So strikingly did her profile resemble my mother's that I thought I must still be dreaming. She turned round to face me. It was mother. Rising with my son in her arms, she approached the bed and lowering her burden carefully into the cradle by the bedside took my limp hand in hers. A mother I must have known in infancy had come to stroke clammy hair from my brow, to thank God that my temperature seemed to be down, to tuck bedclothes beneath my chin, to offer me a drink of lemonade. Astounded, I asked her how on earth she came to be there.

'Don't you realize,' she said, with a hint of her old tartness, 'how ill you have been? Gibson sent for me. He was almost on the verge of a collapse himself when I arrived.'

I asked her what she thought of her grandson, and she admitted he was a fine boy. He looked more like a three-month old than a week. As he was a month overdue and weighed over twelve pounds at birth it was small wonder bringing him into the world had nearly cost me my life.

I pondered on this in silence for a moment and then remarked dreamily in a way that seemed to annoy her that I supposed no one died till his hour had come.

She said that I had to thank my doctor that I was alive. So profuse was the haemorrhage at the afterbirth that if he had not staunched the flow with his naked fist, I'd have bled to death. He had been calling twice a day to give me injections for puerperal fever which, Gibson said, was due to the midwife's negligence. He accused her of failing to sterilize the doctor's instruments properly, and she left in a huff, threatening to sue both him and Dr Blair for libel. It was a relief to be rid of her.

Although my breasts ached with milk, the doctor would not allow me to feed Michael until my temperature had been normal for twenty-four hours. He arrived to superintend the event, armed with a magnificent bunch of flowers. He shyly presented me with the pick of his garden. I buried my face gratefully in the roses, mignonette, clove pinks, and, best of all, what must have been the last of his sweetpeas. 'Isn't it enough, doctor,' complained mother, 'that you've saved her life without robbing your garden of its best for her benefit?'

He replied that only the best was good enough for such a plucky woman.

The moment I had been looking forward to had arrived at last. My son, scarlet in the face, and battling blindly against the constricting mesh of the shawl, nosed straight for the nipple. Alas, the more vigorously he attacked, the more acute the pain, and the worst of it was he failed to draw a drop. My distress brought tears to my eyes.

'Don't give up. Be patient. Try again,' encouraged Dr Blair. He told me how to cup a breast firmly beneath a hand. No sooner did I do so than a spurt of milk fountained from the nipple straight into his eyes.

'You've drowned and blinded me,' he said, laughing, and mopping his brow. 'Give that supply to the boy, don't waste it on me.'

I guided my son's fumbling lips and sure enough his yells subsided as nuzzled against a breast, he began to draw the milk rhythmically in great greedy gulps. When he'd had enough he looked up drowsily into my face with a beatific expression. I have had no experience quite so satisfying as to have my baby feed contentedly from my breast. My happiness was complete.

Not until the end of her life did I feel so close to my mother as I did during the month she stayed with us in Hale. I learnt from her how to handle Michael in his bath, how to change him, how to distinguish a cry of hunger from one of protest. Gibson called her the Queen Bee. Her buzzing filled the house. No-one could be more entertaining than she when she tried. Her racy humour and her acid remarks on the eccentricities and failings of others were a delight when they were not at my expense. In spite of having to sleep on the settee in the back parlour, she never complained. She bought a rocking-chair, and a second hand pram.

All my mother needed, Gibson thought, to make her a contented instead of a sour woman, was simply ordinary human affection and understanding. The women my father surrounded himself with at White Lodge were enough to drive any woman crazy. Jealousy and frustration were her trouble. He was right, I suppose.

Apart from a few words over the hedge with our neighbour, a pretty grass widow whose husband was a prisoner of war, I had no-one to talk to all day after my mother had gone.

Wanting the revered Dr Brodsky to be godfather to Michael and to show him off, Gibson wheeled him one Sunday morning in the clumsy, badly-sprung pram, two and a half miles to Bowdon and back. On the way home he stopped at a pub, and so was not only late for dinner himself but made Michael late for his. I could hear him way down the road, and rushing out of the house to rescue him from the pram it made me even more furious to find his father dawdling flirtatiously at the gate with the woman next door. Ignoring her, I scolded him; and as I crossly pushed the pram to the door, I heard him complain he was henpecked.

'You women,' he said, sidling up to her, 'are artful: sweet as pie before marriage. Once you've got your man trapped you quickly turn sour. I don't trust one of you.'

'Nor do I trust men,' she responded with a provocative laugh that incensed me as much as what he'd said.

The reverberations of the October Revolution finally reached our sluggish life in Hale. I rejoiced in it. It was all mixed up with Ireland for me. The storming of the Winter Palace by the Bolsheviks was like a personal success; the revolution a victory over my enemies in New York: the triumph of the dispossessed like the immigrants with whom I'd travelled steerage. Many of them had been warned by American bosses at factory gates: 'No Irish need apply.'

Gibson shared my dislike of the Czar but approved of the Kerensky Government and its decision to continue the war. He thought it right for Russia to stand by her allies. I didn't, and we began to argue politics. To me, Lenin was right. Should the Bolsheviks succeed in disengaging the Russian people from the capitalist struggle for power, it would hasten the end of a war which every single thoughtful European hated.

Gibson rounded on me. I didn't know what I was talking about. The Bolsheviks were in a minority. For a minority to dictate to the majority was a tyranny as bad as the Czar's. And Russia would be plunged into a civil war which was a catastrophe to be avoided at all costs.

'At the cost of the revolution being crushed by the privileged classes, backed by the Allies?' I asked heatedly.

I remember snatching a paper from him when, tired and dispirited, he returned from his dreary work one bleak, autumnal evening. 'See!' I shouted, pointing to a headline. 'Kerensky's cadets are sniping from roof tops on the workers in the streets. What price your Provisional Government now?'

'Is supper ready?' he demanded to know.

'No regular army, no army of conscripts but ordinary people like ourselves — workers from factories, peasants, deserters from the front, are lying dead and wounded in the streets of Moscow. And all you think about is your stomach.'

'You'd make a good soap-box orator. You're wasting your talents,' he said sarcastically.

'The Russian people,' I shouted, 'are making history — a history that will change the world.'

'Bravo!' he applauded.

'Even now, as you warm yourself by your own fireside, thousands are marching under a stormy sky to the Kremlin, shouting slogans, singing revolutionary songs. Countless red banners wave in the wind, turning the great square into a vast field of poppies. It's wonderful — inspiring.'

'I wish it would inspire you to dish up the stew,' he grumbled. 'I'm starving.'

I think my outburst was some kind of protest against the restrictions imposed by marriage on a woman who wanted to be free to follow her destiny even though she didn't know what it was.

'That's right,' he scoffed good-humouredly, as I wept with

anger. 'Turn on the waterworks, and put an end to the firework display. Give an old horse, in harness all day, some fodder.' He smiled and I felt ashamed of myself.

9   To Moscow?

With a return of the summer which had heralded the coming of my son, I received a surprising letter from Aunt Louisa. Feeling it her duty, she had left The Peak to join the staff of a Military Hospital at York and was at present spending a week's rest with old acquaintances of hers from Dublin, at Congleton in Cheshire, near enough to Hale to enable us to meet. She could come to Hale. But she'd prefer it if I'd spend a day with her and the Miss Pearsons.

Rather than have her inspect the shortcomings of our home, I arranged that Gibson should look after Michael on the following Saturday. As I had not left the house for a whole year, except to go shopping with Michael in the pram, it was up to him to give me a day to myself. He agreed and said that should he get into difficulties about Michael's meals, he could always call on the lady next door to lend a hand.

'In that blue frock you're wearing you don't look a day more than sweet seventeen. Mind you behave yourself!'

'The same goes for you. A merry grass widow is more tempting than three old maids.'

On getting off the train from Manchester to Congleton, the qualms I had at deserting my son on his first birthday disappeared completely. The air scented by new mown hay that reached the sanded platform bordered by flowerbeds and a hedge of briar rose went to my head. The girl I'd left behind in Ireland dawdled through the sleepy little town to arrive all too soon at a substantial Victorian house in a tree-lined avenue.

My aunt had been watching my approach from a window and flung open the door in welcome. She held me at arm's length and examined me with her bright bird's eyes. I was too thin by far.

Was I getting enough to eat? Or was I giving all my nourishment to that boy? She'd heard from my mother that it was hard to make ends meet. And who's fault was that, she'd like to know? My mother's, for allowing me to marry a penniless musician and a Colonial into the bargain? If she'd had her way she would have sent the young man back where he belonged. 'Take no notice of me,' she said, as I began inventing excuses to get away after lunch. 'I have a sharp tongue in my head, as you know to your cost. Let's forget it and make the most of today.'

The prominent blue veins on the hand that poured me out a liberal helping of sherry in the dining room revealed her age as much as the grey in her hair and her sagging chin.

She admitted sadly that the best of her life lay behind her. She said she did not regret having put The Peak up for auction. Her work for the patients at the hospital, many of whom would be permanently disabled, had been so much appreciated that she had been offered a permanent appointment. The handsome retirement pension she'd get, together with the money she received from the sale of The Peak, would be enough to keep her in comfort in her old age. Mr Emerson, she added shyly, had left The Peak just before the declaration of war, and she had heard nothing from him since.

I was relieved when she left me to do myself up in the bath-room. I regretted having come. Unsure which of the closed doors in the hall was that of the dining-room, I entered a sitting-room by mistake. Outside the open French window was a well-tended lawn, flower beds, and in a herbaceous border a clump of oriental poppies. They drew me to the garden, and I had crossed the room to go out when I saw a young man, his dark hair glistening in the sun, stepping briskly across the lawn towards me. On seeing me, he paused, his head and shoulders silhouetted sharply against the blue sky. Our eyes met. We looked at one another in silence for a timeless moment. I felt I had been travelling to meet him all my life. He flashed white teeth at me. Could it be love at first sight which made his face so familiar?

'You live here?' I managed to stammer.

'Perforce,' he replied, with a shrug. 'I am a pauvre Belgian refugee, the protégé of the good ladies of the house. My name is Fichzon. And you? You are Mees Fitzpatrick's niece, eh?'

I nodded, and for something to say complimented him on his English. Happiness surged through me when he extended a hand

and said, 'Come out into the sunshine.' My aunt bustled into the room. She wondered where I had got to. Lunch was ready. Addressing Fichzon she introduced me unnecessarily as her niece, Mrs Gibson Young. It was a bit like Mr Emerson over again. His eyes clouded. 'Meeses,' he repeated slowly, scowling at the carpet. Turning to me for corroboration, he asked incredulously, 'You are married?'

I was about to say 'I'm afraid so,' when my aunt butted in again and assured him that not only was I well and truly married but that I had a son a year old, a fine boy by all accounts, who did me justice.

'Really?' he said, bowing ironically. 'Congratulations.'

I was so conscious of him at lunch that it spoilt my appetite for the roast duck, green peas, new potatoes, and strawberries fresh from their garden that the Miss Pearsons had provided. Whilst he chatted amicably to the younger of the two sisters who dimpled into smiles whenever he addressed her affectionately as 'Ma chère tante', Aunt Louisa seemed so bent on displaying me to the elder Miss Pearson (or him?) as the devoted domesticated little wife and mother that I was obliged to act the part. When I caught his eye a tacit understanding immediately wiped away the image of myself I was creating for her approval. It wasn't real for him. He saw the self I wanted him to see. An exchange of glances liberated me. I sparkled. I was like an adolescent schoolgirl.

Fichzon suggested we should have coffee in the garden; and as he busied himself serving it the young Miss Pearson, drawing her camp chair close to where I squattered on the grass, started singing his praises. 'The dear boy' would leave a gap in their lives they would find it difficult to fill, should he leave, as he intended, as soon as he received permission from the Home Office to work in this country. He had been trained as an electrical engineer and if not that his knowledge of languages — he spoke French and German better than English — should enable him to find a job as a foreign correspondent in any large industrial firm. It was no wonder he resented being dependent on the money granted to them for his keep by the Committee for the Relief of Refugees. He had made himself so useful about the house, to say nothing of the amount of work he had put in in the garden, that he had more than earned the pocket money they added.

While I listened the shadows lengthened on the lawn. I was

sad to think how soon the perfect afternoon would be over and I be gone. As though guessing my thought, Fichzon sprang to his feet, collected the coffee cups, and approaching my aunt, asked her permission to take me for a walk.

'Take her for a walk! She's come to spend the day with me.'

'For an hour; while you enjoy a siesta in the garden.'

'Let them go,' pleaded the younger Miss Pearson. 'The exercise will do them good and bring some colour to your niece's cheeks.'

Fichzon lost no time. He said right away that my hair was like the gold of the corn, rippling like a tawny sea up to distant woods, or something of the sort. The song of a lark ascending from its nest in the stubble seemed to echo in my heart. As if to lay claim to me, he plucked from between my lips a corn stalk to place it in his own. His eyes changed colour to match his surroundings: indoors they had been nightshade, under open sky indeterminate blue, in the shade of the beeches green. The swarthiness of his skin, his prominent cheekbones, his brow swept by black hair, the Asiatic glitter, reminded me of a gypsy. His hollow cheeks belied the strength of his jaw. He looked tough. I asked if he had gypsy blood in his veins. 'I am certainly a nomad,' he said, spitting out the straw from between his teeth. 'I have no settled home.'

Had he served in the Belgian army? No? How had he escaped conscription? He parried. He questioned me. What did I think of the Russian revolution?

I told him without hesitation that I thought the revolution had almost justified the war. 'I agree,' he said gravely, taking my hand. As hand in hand we retraced our steps across a field of buttercups he explained haltingly that before the war he had been a foreign correspondent to a commercial bank in Brussels. The communists with whom he lodged shared his objection to fighting in an imperialist war. His knowledge of English had proved useful. He had acted as interpreter to an official on the Committee for the Relief of Belgian Refugees, and it was he who used his influence to have him and his friends offered hospitality in England.

He had arrived, penniless, at a camp run by Quakers near Manchester from which he had eventually been rescued by the Miss Pearsons. What had happened to his family? Had he communicated with them since he left home? He had been separated from his people for a year or two before the war. Fortunately they lived far enough from the fighting not to cause him undue anxiety. He intended to return home as soon as conditions made it possible to travel.

'Here's all the gold I have to offer you,' he said, handing me a bunch of buttercups. 'I have travelled a long way to meet you today at Congleton.'

He came to the station to see me off. Pacing the platform, he told me that as soon as his work permit came through he intended to apply to Westinghouse for a job. With any luck his letter of recommendation from the bank might get him taken on as a foreign correspondent either in London or Manchester.

'Try Manchester,' I urged. 'My husband is on the clerical staff at Old Trafford.'

'Bon!' he said, squeezing my arm. 'Fixed. I try Manchester first. Your aunt has your address? Yes? Alors, it's au revoir.'

I no longer dreaded the arrival of the train that was to part me from him.

The guilt that sealed my lips about Fichzon, with whom I'd fallen in love, or imagined I had, demanded I should behave better than ever towards Gibson and Michael. They profited by my loss. By treacherously imagining Fichzon was embracing me in bed, I surprised and satisfied Gibson. But as autumnal gales swept the last leaves from the trees all that was left from that summer day in Congleton was the memory of eyes gazing into mine and a dazzling smile. Gibson made the difference. He met Fichzon at the Works Canteen, and in kindness to a foreigner living on his own in digs at Old Trafford invited him without warning or consulting me to come to tea with us on the following Sunday. When he described Fichzon as a lively, good-looking little bloke who spoke English fluently and who didn't appear to have made friends with the other fellows on the clerical staff and who'd accepted his invitation with an alacrity which proved him to be lonely, I felt thoroughly ashamed of myself. It was as I'd hoped and planned for.

The Sunday proved to be one of those dead November days when nature seems to be asphyxiated. There was a grey mist outside the kitchen window. We were just finishing lunch when a loud knock on the door announced his arrival. It was earlier than I'd expected. To hide the blush that flamed my cheeks I rushed into the scullery to wash Michael's hands and face. Instead of showing Fichzon into the back parlour as I'd asked he brought him into the disordered kitchen. I was never a tidy woman.

Removing his beret, he displayed hair sleeked down by brilliantine. Miserably conscious of my soiled apron, untidy hair, a smudge on my cheek, I made Michael in my arms the excuse for ignoring the hand he offered to me. Instead I said sullenly, 'You've come rather earlier than we expected, Mr Fichzon. The place is in a mess.'

'Don't worry,' he said, removing a smart overcoat. 'I'm happy to be received en famille.' Michael eyed him critically with the gravity of a judge and although he received a friendly pat on the head he stuck his thumb in his mouth, scowled and buried his face in my shoulder. When Gibson left us for a minute to put a match to the parlour fire he said, 'Your son doesn't think much of me.'

'He's shy,' I explained. 'And no wonder. In that suit you're wearing, you look as much out of place in our dirty kitchen as would a naval officer.' 'You flatter me,' he said. 'You don't expect a foreign correspondent to look like a tramp. C'est comme il faut, comprenez, to dress for the job.'

'My husband doesn't bother.'

'Your husband as a musician,' he said with a sardonic twist to his lips, 'enjoys poetic licence.'

Michael made a nuisance of himself at tea. Apart from beating endlessly on a tin tray with a spoon he scattered his cereal all over the tablecloth, spilt a mug of milk on Fichzon's knee and howled when I scolded him. Gibson burnt the toast. The two men talked Westinghouse. The meal was an agony to me; and when Gibson began teasing Fichzon about the typists in his office who had a crush on him I was glad to leave the table to put my son to bed. As if on purpose to thwart my desire to rejoin Fichzon, Michael kept me chained to his cot for the best part of an hour by persistently refusing to settle down to sleep. Not that I missed much. For the remainder of the evening I was obliged to listen to a heated political discussion in which Fichzon began by criticizing the terms of the Peace Treaty with Russia and ended with a fierce attack on the Allies for sending armies of intervention into the Ukraine to help Deniken and his men crush the Red Army. 'Their effort is as futile,' he concluded emphatically, 'as trying to put out a prairie fire with a hose.'

When he left I lit the gas mantle. The gas in the windowpane was reflected as light suspended in darkness; and it occurred to me as I drew the curtains that the reality of my married life had as successfully banished the illusion I had cherished that I meant more to Fichzon than a relief from the company of two fond old maids as the drawn curtains banished the illusion of light. Believing that I was nothing more to him than a passing fancy, I discouraged Gibson's suggestion that we should invite him again, and this despite my sense of irreparable loss.

I tried to give him up in my mind until a wet Monday morning when I ran into him at the back door as I rushed indoors with a bundle of washing I had taken from the line in the garden.

'Good heavens,' I gasped, the colour flooding my cheeks. 'What brought you here at this time of day? Have you been given the sack?'

He took the washing out of my hands, motioned me indoors, and following, tossed the bundle on the kitchen table. His swarthy complexion was ruddied by the fire in the range as it had been by the sunlight. To conceal my nervousness, I ordered him to tell me what had happened. Why wasn't he at the office? If he aired his views at Westinghouse as he had to us the other evening he was bound to lose his job. With one of his heart-warming smiles he assured me he knew his friends from his enemies.

As I tugged at the knot in a red worker's handkerchief with white spots which I used to keep my hair tidy when doing housework, he stayed my hand. 'Leave it on — please,' he entreated. 'It suits you. You look so like a Russian girl that I feel I am back home.'

What did he mean? I thought his home was in Belgium. 'My home,' he replied, retaining my hand, 'is with those who make me feel at home. Right now, it is with a fair, blue-eyed girl whose lips turn up at the corners when she smiles. She reminds me of a girl I left behind, years ago, in Rostov-on-Don.'

'My word,' I teased, 'you do get around! A girl in every port of call, and as many as you like to pick and choose from at Westinghouse, I'll be bound. What about those two in your department? Do you know that they refer to you in private as Rudolph Valentino?'

'Oh,' he shrugged with a gesture of dismissal, 'they are stupid. No esprit, no élan. I might as well go around with a stuffed doll. Either I get the girl I want, or I do without. Understand?'

Instead of acknowledging his meaning I concentrated on sorting out the washing, and as I hung nappies to dry on a rack above the range he explained he had taken the morning off to remove his belongings from his rooms at Old Trafford to a more comfortable place at Altrincham. Altrincham, he added, also had the advantage of being nearer Hale.

Clasping my wrist he drew me to him and with a tenderness that tempted me to sink into his arms he traced with a finger tip the contour of my lips.

'What are you trying to do?' I asked. 'Mesmerize me?'

'If you don't satisfy that thirsty mouth of yours,' he warned, 'it will become hard. Are you happily married?'

'What business is that of yours?'

'I'm not here on business. Are you?' he persisted.

'As happy, I suppose, as most married people are who have to live on three quid a week.' I was turning away to continue my work when he ordered me to look him in the eyes.

I turned to him as one does to the sun. Dark, and glittering with a reflected pin-point of flame, his eyes held me captive. A faint smile curved his lips.

'Bon!' he said, buttoning his overcoat. 'I have my answer. Au revoir.'

I was right in believing au revoir a promise of return. He called regularly once or twice a week. Gibson was keeping up his music. He was conducting a small orchestra composed of amateur musicians at the Works. On the evenings he was out at rehearsals he appeared to encourage rather than to object to Fichzon keeping me company. We did not dare to kiss. To be together was sufficient. He brought with him the Everyman editions of Russian novels. Seated opposite each other at the kitchen table, he read aloud, to improve his English and my knowledge of Russia, scenes from Dostoevsky's *Crime and Punishment*. I identified myself with Sonia, the saintly little prostitute. Fichzon with Raskolnikov, the tragic hero. Charged with an emotion that brought a lump to my throat, I believed myself to be as ready as Sonia to sacrifice a ruined life by following my love to the ends of the earth.

I led a double life. Michael knew it. He was not so easily deceived as his father. To punish me, he became increasingly fractious and demanding. If I turned my back on him for a minute he'd wriggle out of the strap of his high chair or pram and scare me by standing on the edge poised for an imminent fall.

Guilt made me refrain from scolding him. Gibson accused me of spoiling the boy. Fichzon gave him a gaudily painted wooden self-righting Russian peasant doll on which he took pleasure in venting his spleen. As though aiming a missile at Fichzon he would repeatedly throw *Vanka Stanka* across the room, anxiously watch it crash against table or door and as soon as the doll which was the object of his aggression righted itself, shout with glee. *Vanka Stanka* was perhaps his favourite toy because with it he could express his love-hate relationship to Fichzon with impunity.

Fichzon erected shelves in the sitting room for books, in the kitchen and scullery for pots and pans, dug the garden to sow potatoes and turned a grass plot into a cabbage patch. Gibson complained that he usurped his place as husband. I had a weak answer. He refused to spend time on the improvements I had so often begged him to make. He should not grumble I had asked Fichzon.

The first love I had missed as a girl I found in him. It was what I'd been waiting for, to be drawn between his knees by the fireside of an evening when the house was quiet and to have my head cradled in his arms. Love had taken possession of me. To make love would have been superfluous. A simultaneous smile united us as surely as though we slept together, my eyes as naked to him as my body would have been in bed. Knowing this, he trusted me with the truth about himself. He was no Belgian, but a Russian, born and bred at Rostov, within reach of the waters of the Don. The Steppe he described as endless seas of grassland and of grain flowing as far as the eye could reach and beyond. For printing subversive literature in a disused sawmill on a press belonging to his father — a staunch Social Democrat — and for distributing the pamphlets to fellow students, to railway men, and workers at the docks, he had been in danger of arrest. To escape he had to leave for Moscow; from Moscow he had gone to Brussels where his knowledge of modern languages helped him to find a job. He possessed a Belgian passport under the assumed name of Fichzon by which name he was known to the British CID.

'That's all there is to tell,' he said.

'Except your real name. What is it?'

'Grigory, Alexandrovitch Petrov. Grisha please to you — in private.'

The hypocrisy in the smiles with which we welcomed Gibson must surely have shown; but since, according to Grisha, he was having an affair with the pretty widow next door, whose docile

L.O.—G

femininity must have been a pleasing contrast to me, he treated us with a paternal complacency which eased my guilty conscience. When I confessed as much to Grisha he exploded.

'Your marriage is a farce. The sooner you realize it the better. If you don't love your husband why live with him? You deceive him as the woman next door deceives her absent husband. Kept women, both of you.'

'What do you expect me to do?'

'Be honest. Have the courage of your convictions. Tell your husband the truth.'

Scowling at me, as he heard Gibson's latchkey in the door, he hurriedly left the house. And when he failed to return either that week or the next I was in despair. When I was alone I gave way to black depression. At other times I burned with anger at his desertion. Rage at what I considered his unfair suggestion alternated with fear for him. Distracted by the fear that his identity had been discovered and that he had either been deported to Russia or arrested and that I should never see him again I flung myself on the bed to give way to weeping.

Michael's innocent bewilderment restored me to my senses. In his candid eyes I saw myself as a selfish, wayward woman, unfit to be his mother. For his sake, since he depended utterly on me, I must not allow myself to hanker after the impossible. I must struggle against an attachment which would ruin his happiness. I had at last succeeded in becoming resigned to the inevitable when Gibson informed me that Fichzon had been transferred from the Works at Old Trafford to the offices of Westinghouse in London.

'Has he gone for good?' I enquired with ill-concealed anxiety.

His sarcastic 'For his good or ours?' silenced further questions.

Just before Christmas I received a picture postcard. He wrote that he was enjoying London, where he expected to be for an indefinite period and that he had met my father at the office who, on hearing that he had met me, had invited him to his home at Wimbledon. He found my mother 'sympathique'. His regards to Gibson, kiss to Michael. It stood upon the kitchen mantelpiece for months.

In that first year of a peace that had been paid for at the price of eight and a half million dead and more than twice that number wounded, spring came early to a victorious Britain threatened with economic ruin. To take advantage of the warmth of sun

March offered I was up and out early trundling Michael in his pram to the fields. Returning from one such outing, to escape a sudden shower I pushed the pram so fast that I was obliged to pause for breath at the corner of our street. I saw a man in a black mackintosh propping up the gate. I slackened my pace and had come within a few yards of the house before I recognized Grisha. His arms straddling the gate, he reminded me of a print I had seen of a wounded cavalry officer splayed against his horse's flank on some field of battle in the Napoleonic wars. Stirred by the beauty of his face, pale and wet from rain, I dared not trust myself to speak.

'I come home,' he said, greeting me with the same smile as he had when first we met, 'to find myself locked out.'

I twisted a button on his mac with trembling fingers. I caressed its wet surface.

Disregarding Michael's protesting howl, he took the pram from me and shoved it up the path to the door. In less time than it takes to tell, he had a fire blazing in the kitchen range, set a kettle on the hob, and while I prepared tea, kept Michael contented by helping him construct a house from kindling wood. 'You would make a good husband for the right girl,' I teased. 'And you,' he said, quick to take the cue, 'a good wife for the right man.'

I pestered him with questions about my parents. My father should, in his opinion, have been a diplomat. It was a pity he wasted his talents on a set of sexually disappointed women who flattered his vanity by their devotion. My parents and their entourage had much in common with certain quasi-religious sections of the intelligentsia in Russia before the Revolution. Reformists who refused to recognize the class structure of the society of which they were a privileged part they deceived themselves into believing that socialism could be achieved by gentleman's agreement. My father's liberal opinions suited a democracy, in which a parliamentary system acted as a smokescreen to blind the working class about the true nature of a competitive society.

'Surely,' I protested, 'you didn't tell your political opinions to father?' He had only risked a skirmish.

'And what about mother? You said you found her sympathetic.'

'Your mother treated me like a son. Consequently I adopted her as my mother-in-law.'

I could imagine them sitting close and exchanging confidences, mother, under his spell, telling him about my marriage and he letting the story of my pregnancy confirm his opinion that my marriage had been merely one of convenience.

'What did she say that makes you so pleased with yourself? You're grinning like a cat.'

'Your mother has perception. She thinks I would have suited you better than Gibson.'

'He wouldn't thank her for that,' I remarked dryly. 'What else did she say?'

'She sympathized with us, but said that as there was nothing I could do to alter it now I had best keep my distance. I told her that depended on you. "Don't make Gibson jealous," she warned, and said that if provoked Gibson would find a way of taking you to Australia.'

'She hit the mark. He may.'

'What!' he said, his eyes blazing. 'He can't force you to go without your consent. He's not your keeper, nor you his follower. It's for you to make up your mind what you want to do, and the sooner the better.'

He spoke truculently. I implored him to be reasonable.

'I've been reasonable for too long. There is a limit to my patience. This ménage à trois sickens me. I'm through with it. Understand?'

He emphasized his ultimatum with a snap of his fingers.

'What is the alternative?' I ventured to inquire.

'That is for you to decide. Put the boy to bed — as quickly as possible,' he ordered.

'Your servant, Sir,' I mocked, curtseying to him with Michael in my arms.

On returning to the kitchen there was no sign of him. I called him, looked everywhere for his mac, and, failing to find it, believed he had left to spite me. I slumped into a chair and buried my face in my hands. The back door banged. He entered on a gust of wind, his hair ruffled, his mac shiny with rain.

'I have been weeding the potatoes. If you take the trouble to look after them, you should have a good crop to remember me by when I'm gone.'

'Gone!' I repeated, gaping at him wide-eyed. 'Where? Back to London?'

He seated himself opposite me, lit a cigarette and told me

casually that he expected soon to return to Russia. Though he
had merely confirmed what I had secretly dreaded since the
Armistice, I couldn't bear to think of him being swept away to
a future in which I had no part. I asked how soon he expected
to leave.

By late spring. Probably by May his transit visa would come
through.

'To Rostov? In the midst of the fighting in the Ukraine? You'll
be killed,' I cried with tragic finality. He had work to do for the
revolution as important as joining the Red Army. He was going
to Moscow. At his imperative 'Listen!' I drew my chair nearer.
Our knees touched.

Seated opposite me in his black mac, his damp hair swept
across brows knitted in a frown, his eyes, veiled by luxuriant
lashes, watched me closely as he offered me a preposterous plan.
But he meant what he said. If I would agree to live with him either
at Altrincham or in London until such time as he was ready to
leave for Moscow he would be able, with the aid of a contact in
Russia, to obtain a visa for me that would permit me to join him
in Moscow as his wife. In Soviet law union by consent constituted
a marriage.

'You would be able,' he urged, 'to build in a socialist society
a new life on the ruins of your old, Edite (that is how he always
pronounced my name). Danielovna Petrov, citizen of the Soviet
Union! Risk it. The hour of truth has arrived. Tell your
husband you love me and want to live with me. End the hypocrisy once and for all.'

The smile that transfigured his face was an enthusiastic boy's.
He was as childish at heart as I was, and have remained, or more
so.

'Sounds tempting,' I admitted, but I was only trying to humour
him.

To tempt me further he said he had heard from a reliable
source that housing conditions had improved lately and that life
in many respects had returned to normal in Moscow and Lenin-
grad. Extras could be bought on the blackmarket, cafés in both
capitals were crowded, the theatres full. By mentioning a café
in the *Tverskaya,* famous as a rendezvous for artists and writers,
where Mayakovsky read his poems to his admirers, he made it
all seem more real. I imagined dawn breaking over the waters of
the Neva and mass demonstrations celebrating victories of the

Red Army in the south. He suggested that I should add to our income by teaching English. That was too realistic. It recalled me to myself.

'You've forgotten the main obstacle. You've forgotten Michael,' I reminded him. 'I couldn't, I wouldn't desert my son.'

He pondered on this for a moment. Of course I must bring him too. He was fond of the boy, and would treat him as his own son.

'And what about Gibson? Do you think he'd agree to part with his son? He adores Michael. If I were to leave him, he could claim custody, take Michael with him to Australia and I'd never see him again. I couldn't bear it. It would break my heart.'

'Hearts,' he sneered 'are not so easily broken as bones — except in novelettes.'

Flinging my hand from his knee he began pacing the room. He thought better of Gibson than I did. He didn't believe he would be so mean as to hold Michael hostage to bind me to a marriage contract which meant so little to him that he had already broken it himself by making love to the woman next door. He had seen him on more than one occasion when he was supposed to be at rehearsals sneaking out of her back door. For a wife to excuse her husband's infidelities to cover up her own made a mockery of a marriage that had been doomed to failure from the start.

'I assure you,' he said, turning on me savagely, 'it is only a matter of time before your husband leaves you, or you leave him. Either you'll have to support yourself — and your son — on the amount of alimony you can squeeze from a reluctant husband, or earn your own living. And as you're not the kind of woman to be content on your own, you will either marry again or take lovers.'

'Why the plural?' I asked.

'Because you will always be looking for a perfection you will never find. When you're old you'll be left in some shabby back room consoling yourself with romantic memories of a lost youth.'

'Enough!' I shouted at him. 'The future is what we make it. The picture you've been painting of mine shows what you think of me.'

'I think enough of you to ask you to share my life.'

'And what a life! Exile in a country ravaged by civil war.'

'In the end,' he reflected slowly, 'security, or what she believes to be security, is more important to a woman than love. I am a fool to have thought you an exception.'

He had never been more dear to me than when, buttoning his mac, he said goodbye in a tone of finality that seemed like a death sentence. I rushed after him, caught him up at the scullery door, and, clutching his mac like a beggar, implored him not to go. In the light of the gas jet above the sink his eyes searched mine.

'I can't bear to part from you, I love you, Grisha.'

'Prove it,' he commanded. Flinging my arms round his neck, I tenderly pressed my lips to his face. Clasping me to him, he covered my mouth with his in a kiss that enticed me to melt into so close an embrace that I knew no difference between myself and him.

Neither of us noticed that the back door had opened nor that Gibson blocked his exit to the windy night. Seizing Grisha by the scruff of the neck he hurled him with the strength of rage against the lintel of the door.

'Out, you scoundrel!' he panted. 'If you come within sight of this house again, I'll call the police. I'll have you arrested for seducing my wife, you sneak, you traitor.'

'Abuse won't get you anywhere,' sneered Grisha, tensing as though to spring at him. Thinking better of it, he shrugged disdainfully and sauntered out into the darkness. White with fury myself, I pushed past Gibson and ran after him.

'Quick, your address. What is it?' I repeated it after him. 'Near the gas works,' he called after me. 'Come soon, *moen gopoion.*' A Russian endearment I did not understand reached me on the wind.

I reluctantly returned to face my husband. He was in his shirt sleeves making cocoa. We avoided looking at each other. Neither spoke, until in anger I burst out. 'Your vulgarity astounded me. You behaved like a caveman, a brute.'

'And you,' he returned, 'like a cheap little tart.'

'Your tart is next door,' I reminded him.

'Who's being vulgar now?'

Insult capped insult, mounting to a crescendo of recrimination. If he saw that scruffy little Belgian hanging round the place again he'd murder him. I threatened to divorce him because of our neighbour.

'Your misconduct,' he retorted, 'needs no proof. I could divorce you on the strength of it.'

'Go ahead then, do. It's what I want.'

'Go to your lover, I'll not stop you. But you're not taking my son. I'm keeping Michael. I have the law on my side.'

'I'm not leaving him to the care of your mistress.'

'Nor I to the care of that bloke of yours. I'd see myself dead first.'

There was a silence in which I dissolved in tears. Relenting, he stole behind me to lay a hand on the nape of my neck. So vividly did the gesture recall the sensation of a hand laid on my neck the evening before Michael was born that it acted like a shock. Shuddering, I looked up at him.

'Mimi,' he said tenderly, 'I am as much to blame as you. Let us forgive and forget.'

I could find no answer; nor when he took my arm to lead me up to bed could I offer resistance.

Bitterly as I resented my husband's treatment of Grisha, I could not honestly blame him. I recognized he had a legitimate excuse but I could still make no effort to bridge the gulf between us. We behaved to each other as strangers, occupying the same house. That the fatal decision rested with me, rather than proving a spur, paralysed me. I started at every unusual sound, and lived in constant expectation of either meeting Grisha by chance in the street or of his taking the risk of calling at the house. Time and again I rushed to the gate in the hope that a passing footstep might be his. Should I see anyone remotely resembling him alight from a bus when I was out shopping with Michael, I would rush the pram to the bus stop. Tempted though I was to seek him out, fear that it would mean total capitulation held me back.

I could not make up my mind and became ill. I had 'flu when a letter arrived from my brother asking whether he could rent our front room for himself and Flora.

My father had found him a job in a printing firm near Manchester which specialized in lithography and although as an apprentice he would not be earning enough to support Flora they intended to get married on her allowance. They would have enough to share household expenses and pay half the rent; from the oddments passed on to Flora from her parents' home, they would have plenty to furnish their room. As they were anxious to move in as early as possible, would I reply by return to White Lodge, where they hoped to spend part of their honeymoon. Gibson welcomed the proposal both on financial grounds and because it would give us companionship we liked. I feared the presence of a sister-in-law in the house would seem like an intrusion. I was wrong.

Perhaps because she flattered me at the outset by remarking to my brother that I reminded her of Botticelli's Primavera I took to Flora at once. Her candid blue eyes invited confidence. An abundance of glossy black hair swept from a low forehead to a bun at the nape of her neck redeemed a thin upper lip and receding chin. An ample figure supported that proud head; and in the loose flowing garments she favoured she gave the impression of floating rather than walking. My brother said she waddled. 'She's my fine fat duck,' he would say, fondly nibbling at her cheek.

I kept my distance from the happy couple as much as the house allowed. Their absorption in each other made me feel cynical. I never entered their room unless invited. I left it to Flora to interrupt me in the kitchen should she feel inclined to whilst awaiting Ronald's return from work. She surprised me one afternoon when I was in the middle of washing nappies by remarking that she had noticed a constraint between Gibson and myself which worried her.

'It's more than a constraint,' I confessed impulsively. 'It's an armed truce. I've fallen in love with somebody else.'

'Are you sure,' she said, fixing me with those great eyes of hers as though to read my soul, 'are you sure it's love?'

'Whatever it is, it tortures me. I haven't a moment's peace.'

'I should have thought,' she considered, her lips twitching, 'that like Ronald you had enough of the artist in you to be incapable of becoming totally involved in another. I have no wish to probe but sometimes it's a relief to confide in someone you can trust.'

Could I trust her not to tell Ronald if I confided in her? She had no secrets from Ronald, but would not volunteer unless specially invited. Any love, she believed, was only as strong as its weakest link and until the strength of that link had been tested there was no guarantee that love would last.

The temptation to ask her advice was so strong that later in the evening I knocked on the door of a room in which a few good, solid pieces of furniture had worked wonders. There were turkish rugs on an oak stained floor and a double divan. An ultramarine wallpaper made a fitting background for a portrait of Flora. Sitting at her knee I told her all that was in my heart, omitting nothing in the story. She listened carefully. She criticized Fichzon, saying it was dishonest to pass himself off as a Belgian refugee when he was in reality a Russian and should by rights be in Russia.

'That's beside the point,' I snapped impatiently. 'His Belgian passport provides him with a work permit without which he would have either to starve or scrounge. He intends returning to Russia soon and I have to decide whether to go with him or stick to Gibson.'

Unless I sought my own happiness or what I believed to be happiness at the price of bringing suffering to others she did not think I had a choice. I quailed from her eyes and from the voice of duty.

'Duty,' I said attacking her, 'is a poor substitute for love. It breeds resentment that can easily turn to hatred.'

'As I see it,' she reflected, 'what you should do is decide which of these three who lay claim on you means most to you.'

Without a moment's hesitation I said, 'My son.'

'In that case,' she replied, clasping my hand, 'you've solved your problem. You must do what is best for him.'

As I let the obvious sink in, she said something she shouldn't. She understood from Ronald that Gibson had written to his father asking him to cable by return our passage money to Australia.

'*Our* passage?' I repeated, rounding on her indignantly, 'What cheek to take for granted that I shall go with him.'

'He does apparently.'

'He has no right to decide my future without first consulting me.'

'Gibson has as much right to try to find a solution as you have,' she rebuked gravely.

'Before that I'm going to see Grisha.'

'Is that wise?' she questioned.

'It's a must,' I said, flinging aside the hand which sought to detain me.

I rushed out of the house, hatless, in my working clothes, and streaked like lightning down the road through the streets of Altrincham to the address I thought I knew by heart. Distant smoke coming from the chimney of a gas works led me to a street of dreary houses, each separated from the pavement by area railings. At each flight of steps, alike as teeth in a false set, I searched each uninviting door for the number I was after. I couldn't find it. I crossed and recrossed the road and was giving up in despair when in an end house I caught sight of Grisha in a blue shirt bending over a table in a bow-window writing. Before my trembling fingers had reached the bell he was at the door. Grasping me by the arm he pulled me across the hall.

'Better late than never,' he remarked. 'Sit down, I'll make tea.'

'I can't stay long, Grisha. I've left Michael to the care of my sister-in-law and she handles him like a china doll.'

Asked what she was doing there I falteringly explained, adding that as Gibson had refused to let me have custody of Michael and was preparing to return to Australia I had no alternative but to go with him.

He thrust his jaw at me like a pugilist. His lips parted in a snarl.

'Why,' he asked, clearing his throat, 'did you look me up? You should have saved yourself the trouble.'

'I had to see you again to tell you that I can't leave Michael. To explain.'

'You are mine, not your husband's,' he said approaching me menacingly. 'To live with him is living a lie. I may not have much to offer you, but all I have is yours.'

He looked pathetic standing there, his shirt sleeves rolled to the elbows, young, vulnerable, thin — almost gaunt. The prominence of his wrists went with the prominence of his cheekbones. My heart ached as much for him as for myself.

'I'm afraid you've been neglecting yourself. Have you been eating properly?'

'Either you love me, or you don't. If you don't, get out,' he ordered harshly, flinging open the door.

'Grisha, please try to understand.'

'I understand perfectly. You are afraid to risk life with me and you use your son as an excuse. Bonjour, Madame.'

It didn't take me long to slip into the hall and out of the house. He came running down the steps after me. I took to my heels. Panting, he caught me up. His hair was streaked across his eyes. He pinioned me to an area railing.

'People are staring at us. Let go of me,' I said, struggling in his grasp.

'Listen. You have come just in time. I can arrange for you to join me in London next week. I give you one more chance to decide. Now or never.'

'Oh Grisha darling,' I cried in distress, 'Please don't ask me to repeat what I've already said. I cannot abandon Michael.'

'You cheat yourself,' he retorted in scorn. 'Self sacrifice is not your métier. You're not in love with me. You're in love with a love affair. Bien, you've had it. Bon voyage.'

Freeing me, he put his hands in his pockets and sauntered back with a characteristic swagger down the road. I stood looking after him, tears streaming down my cheeks, until he had disappeared into the house. I knew that now I had said goodbye to him forever.

As soon as Gibson got the cable from his father promising him a sum of money far exceeding his expectations he had begun planning. After a weekend in London to say goodbye to my parents we were to leave for Southampton to embark for New York and from there to see Niagara Falls, cross the continent on the Canadian Pacific, stop a few days in the Rockies and thence to Vancouver to wait for the boat for Sydney. The detailed arrangements for so lengthy a journey with a young child acted as a counter-irritant to the pain of the final parting from Grisha. The agents had agreed to my brother's taking over the remainder of our lease so the house was to be his for another year.

In the dark hall in the grey light of early morning I clung, sobbing, to Flora. My brother stood on one side, nervously running his hand through his silky beard.

'Think of me, Flora, and write. I'll be hungry for news of home.'

'And I for news of you, my sister,' she said holding me to her breast. 'You have become very dear to me.'

'Hey, hey,' objected my brother. 'No more of that. You're making me jealous.'

At Gibson's call from a waiting taxi I ran down the garden path. At the gate I turned round to wave to the pair framed by the door of the house which I had prayed for.

This time we didn't have to share a cabin amongst other immigrants in the bowels of the ship. We enjoyed the luxury of a cabin to ourselves on the boat deck of a half empty liner, one of a convoy escorted by mine-sweepers across the Atlantic. In the compact, rattling box, safe from waves lashing spray on the port-hole, I lay and splashed green bile into a container fixed to the bunk. Once over it, Gibson helped me to a camp-chair sheltered behind a life boat from the wind. My eyes on the sky, I turned inwards to think about the past and in particular about the harrowing weekend I had spent with my parents at White Lodge.

Michael had refused to let me out of his sight. My mother accused me of fussing far too much over him.

'Make him independent of you. Smack him when he whines,' she ordered. 'If you don't you'll turn him into a spoilt brat, a burden to you, and a trouble to Gibson's parents.'

Not content with upsetting me by criticizing Michael, whose behaviour I explained as insecurity at being wrenched from his own home, she started attacking Grisha.

'Thank God,' she began, 'Gibson had the sense to send that Fichzon packing before he succeeded in messing up your life. Your father always said he was a shady character but I stood up for him.'

'Oh, I know he had charm,' she replied in response to a mild protest on my part, 'he knew so well how to get round me that I actually invited him to stay here, free of charge, the last time he came to London.'

'Doubtless you knew he was a Russian and shared his political opinions,' she continued, eyeing me suspiciously through her spectacles.

I admitted that I did. What was she getting at?

'In that case, did it ever occur to you that he might be a spy in the pay of the Bolsheviks?' she incensed me by asking.

'Of course not. What rubbish! You don't suppose Westinghouse would have taken him on their clerical staff unless they had been sure he was above suspicion?' I glared at her apprehensively.

'Oh,' she said, 'he was a dark horse. He knew how to wangle things to suit himself. According to Elsie — who, by the way, was also head over ears in love with him — the two detectives from the Foreign Office who called here at midnight when your father and I were sound asleep in bed ransacked his papers in search of incriminating evidence and told Elsie as they ushered him, hatless, and without an overcoat, out of the house, that he was to be deported to Russia as an undesirable alien. Do you know what he had the impudence to say to Elsie as she sobbed on his neck at the door? That it suited him fine to be sent home at the British Government's expense. Typical of the rascal,' she commented with a sigh. I said that if he'd been a spy I would have thought no less of him. Indeed I would have admired him the more for exposing himself to danger for the sake of his convictions.

'You should congratulate yourself that you didn't allow your romantic attachment to come between you and Gibson. I give you credit for that; and I give Gibson credit for giving you an opportunity of starting afresh in Australia. I don't pity any of you. You're young, life is before you. It's myself I'm sorry for, left behind, with nothing to look forward to in the future but old age.'

Grisha's face, haggard as when I had last seen it, rose up before me at every lurch and roll of the liner. I realized that there was some truth in his parting remark. It was not only my concern for my son which had prevented me breaking up my marriage, but an instinct of self-preservation.

'Here comes my salvation army,' I cried, opening wide my arms, as Michael, his hand in the grip of a sailor, came tottering across the deck from the hatch to my shelter. Balancing a tea tray his father followed him.

'O.K. now, sonny boy?' said the kindly sailor, delivering him to me. Gibson, laying the tray on my knee, dislodged Turgenev's *Torrents of Spring* — Grisha's last gift — from the lifebelt which in case the ship accidentally struck an undetected mine, each passenger was obliged to keep by him. 'The tea,' said Gibson, 'may be a bit cold; but after that adulterated bread we've been having for the last four years the white bread and butter is delicious. Taste it.' I needed no persuasion, and as he tucked the rug cosily about my knees I told him in gratitude that he treated me far better than I deserved.

'It's up to a bloke, isn't it,' he replied, with a grin, 'to look after his wife. You've taken nothing solid since we embarked.'

10 Australia Instead

Compared with the effect on me of my childhood in New York, the seven and a half years I spent in Australia seem but a pleasant interlude in which I played at being grown up. I had to: as wife and mother I was reckoned adult. I felt as forlorn as an adopted child amongst so many alien faces.

For the first few months the efforts I made to contact somebody apart from husband and son with whom I could communicate came to nothing. I was critical of all that appeared brash, commonplace, devoid of subtlety, both in the landscape and the people.

I am sure my father-in-law, a frustrated, taciturn man, a hypochondriacal diabetic, couldn't for the life of him understand why Gibson had married a girl who, in his opinion, had nothing to recommend her but her accent. He avoided being alone with me. If he ever was he would either bury his head in a newspaper or bolt from the room. If I expressed an opinion contrary to his on any subject he would respond either with a hostile rebuff or an equally hostile silence. To be indebted to him made me feel much as my mother must have when she had to accept Mrs Lindsay's hospitality in New Jersey. I echoed her — 'the bread of charity leaves a bitter taste in the mouth'. My definition of war as organized mass murder sparked off a row with him that humiliated me still further. He reminded me that I wouldn't be where I was were it not for the war. He had paid for my trip to Australia from his investment in War Bonds.

'Had I known that,' I blazed at him, 'I would have refused to come.'

'Pity you didn't,' he returned coolly. 'It would have saved a lot of expense.'

I told him I'd not trouble him much further. I would look for a job as governess or shop assistant — anything that would enable me to pay for my keep until his son could provide me with a home.

With that I dashed out of the house to wander disconsolately about the suburban streets till nightfall.

Gibson's mother, a timid little woman, who must once have been a pretty and spirited girl, had been so broken in by her demanding husband that she scarce dared speak in his presence. A little speckled hen, she tucked her beak in her feathers when he was there and fussed over Michael and myself in his absence. She was as devoted to her one and only beloved son as her husband was to their youngest daughter.

It was easy to understand why Gibson had left home. There was a gulf between himself and his parents which no effort on either side could ever bridge. Gibson was such an enigma to his mother that in her efforts to please him she invariably did or said the very thing guaranteed to irritate him most effectively.

She told me she knew it was hard on me, blinking at me shyly while I helped her wash up. I should take no notice of Dad. His bark was worse than his bite. Gibson, poor boy, was as anxious as me to be independent. Let's pray he got the job he has applied for at the Melba Conservatorium. In the meantime I should enjoy myself and leave Michael — God bless his little heart — to her and go off on my own to see Melbourne.

She implored me not to look for a job. Her husband wouldn't hear of it, neither would Gibson; rather than humiliate them all I should pocket my pride. As for herself, it was such joy to have me and Michael about the place that she dreaded the day we would leave.

I embraced her. She fluttered in my arms, her bright eyes dimmed by tears. Miriam who was by nature a Martha consigned me quite happily to the role of a Mary. She sent me off on voyages of discovery.

Melbourne, as close to the equator as Athens, must clearly share its clarity of light, sharp shadows, heat tempered by sea breezes. The Victorian dominated the city when I was there. St Pancras Station might well have been the model for many public buildings including the Houses of Parliament. Streets as wide as boulevards, as ramblas, lent spaciousness to the foothills north of the narrow river Yarra. On clear days a range of hills was silhouetted on the horizon.

Surrounding the city proper, beyond the respectability of mansioned Toorak and its adjacent suburbs, there sprawled, uphill and down, a monotonous expanse of redbricked, terra-cotta-roofed villas, and weatherboard bungalows. A lawn, either mean or spacious, with an assortment of trees, flower beds and flowering shrubs, gave a rural privacy to these Australian homes. Gibson's parents' home was like that. My first impression of it was of a show house in an Ideal Home Exhibition, which the rambler roses and bougainvillia covering the veranda did little to dispel. Every blade of grass on the lawn looked in place. Not a weed to be seen in the herbaceous border. Even the tool-shed and dustbins were hidden behind scentless white roses.

Once it got out that the stranger imported into the Young household was of Irish stock all was explained. No wonder I appeared unlike any other Pommy they had come across. To the nonconformist protestants to whom I was initially introduced the Irish, as Catholics, were a race apart and, as rebellious trouble-makers, suspect. These Australians spoke as nostalgically of a trip Home to the Old Country as the provincial characters in Chekhov's plays pining for Moscow. To have been Home conferred a prestige equal to Mecca.

'What marks the changes of season in a country of evergreens?' I asked Gibson. 'I find the monotony of the two hundred species of gum as depressing as the people.'

'Be patient. Once your eye is used to the landscape, you'll find all sorts of subtlety in the bush; it's chiefly the temperature which marks the change of season. There are winter days in Melbourne when you'll regret having left your mother's astrakhan coat behind.'

'I warn you,' he continued severely, 'that as long as you adopt a superior attitude to the Australians, they'll shun you. The one thing they can't stand is a snob.'

'To be a snob is beyond my means.'

'It's not. You're an intellectual snob. But I don't blame you for being bored with the stuffy set of social climbers who hang round my parents.'

A sea washing a stretch of deserted beach; sand dunes; sandy tracks between tee trees, twisted and gnarled, grey-green as olive, surrounded our first home, a ramshackle, old weatherboard house recommended to Gibson for its privacy by its owner, anxious to let it furnished to a reliable tenant, during his absence in New Guinea. He assured Gibson that Parkdale was in easy reach of

Melbourne, and although the house was some distance from the
station he would be able to have a dip in the sea before he set off
to town in the morning.

Tee trees encroached on the wire-netted veranda. Gums
crowded the back door. Footsteps were muffled by sand right up
to the house. My cushions and rugs looked like plumage amongst
the owner's collection of junk from auction rooms and an odd
assortment of family heirlooms. Once we had stowed them in a
back bedroom cupboard and I had displayed our own possessions
the gloomy old house looked a bit better. From the top windows
we could see the sea.

As Michael and I had the time to ourselves we spent each day
on the beach. He paddled about naked with bucket and spade. I
swam out to drift along like a gull. In the hollow of a sand dune
we built an altar to Apollo of driftwood and stones to which we
brought our offering — an odd flower or two which had seeded
themselves in a poor patch of soil at the back of the house, sea
birds' feathers, and the pick of our collection of shells. We
chanted a hymn to the sun god asking him to return at dawn
after he had driven his fiery steeds round about the earth. We
would wait until he had dipped his bright hand beneath the
horizon before returning to the house to prepare Gibson's supper.

As the days shortened I got more upset by the eeriness of the
house at nightfall. I started at each creak of a floorboard, at the
rustle of tee tree on window or netting, at the squeak of mice in a
cupboard. Bored with myself, I felt I was withering fast. I envied
Gibson his life amongst the musicians of Melbourne and resented
his leaving me so much alone. To add to his income as a teacher
he had taken work with an agency as an organizer of parties of
musicians from abroad. He seldom got back to Parkdale, dog
tired and tipsy, till midnight. At breakfast I cursed him before he
went off again. 'You treat me like a caretaker. I won't put up
with it much longer. Unless you find a home in Melbourne for
me, I'll quit anyway and take furnished lodgings in the city. I'm
so much alone I've begun talking to myself.'

He suggested importing as companion a typist from the office
whose husband was away temporarily in Brisbane. It would be
doing his boss a favour, and be good for me. She would be out at
work all day, and company in the evening. On condition that he
would try to sub-let the house for the remainder of the lease I
agreed to the typist.

When she came she was a sulky, mousy-haired girl, whose shortsighted eyes blinked at me through bifocal lenses. 'I don't trust Monica Sharples,' I told Gibson. 'She's sly.'

'Shy,' he corrected. 'Don't you notice how she blushes when you speak to her. She's scared stiff of you.'

'If she is, why does she boast of her conquests? She says there are a couple of men at the office pining for her. Perhaps she imagines you're one.'

'She boasts because she's shy, I suppose. But I'd best steer clear of her. She's ready for anything in trousers.'

Monica had some assets too. Slim, tall, with virginal breasts and taut thighs she shot straight as an arrow from the house each evening when she got home from the office to race across the sand dunes for a plunge in the sea.

One evening when she'd lingered on the beach until moonrise Gibson suggested that while I got the supper he should go and find her. He was gone an hour. I was impatient and set out after them. My feet sank soundlessly into the snow-white sand. I paused within sight of the shore. Then I saw the luminous body of Monica Sharples emerging from the water. Naked, she ran across the beach towards a shadow on the sand. Gibson was waiting there. After a moment, she darted behind a sand dune, presumably to get dressed. Rather than be detected as the witness of what I thought was the finale of a love scene, I swiftly went back to the house.

At supper I asked Gibson whether he too had bathed naked. Monica blushed and looked embarrassed. In the bedroom he came back to it. If I thought he'd been making love to Monica Sharples on the beach I was mistaken. He wouldn't touch her with a barge pole. I suggested he might touch her with a smaller tool. He shook me and said she'd suddenly disappeared to undress behind a sand dune and had then offered herself to him.

'What did you do?'

'She's a bitch,' he said vindictively. 'Bitchy to you and bitchy to her husband. If I'd told her that, she'd have made old Fred believe I'd tried to seduce her.'

'You've sized her up pretty well.'

'Thanks to you,' he said, 'I have. She's a nymphomaniac.'

'All the same I bet you were tempted? You've a weakness for grass widows.'

'Frankly I was,' he admitted, grinning. 'She has a lovely body.

But it wasn't worth the risk. I saw you coming through the scrub, warned her, and she made a dash for the sea. Now she thinks you suspect her, I bet she'll clear out.'

Monica left next day. Gibson sub-let the house to an author of travel books. Gibson had just been appointed musical critic on the Melbourne *Argus*. He was as pleased with that as I was with the spacious flat in a modern block overlooking the Yarra valley that he could now afford. The flat was surrounded by a veranda, part used for sleeping out. It had a view over the city to the hills which deepened from a hazy blue to violet every night before sunset. I used to watch them as I listened to the string quartet in which Gibson played first violin and which he'd invited to rehearse at our flat twice a week.

But I couldn't just act hostess for him and especially not for the star pupil, who played second fiddle to him and whom he was flirting with. I decided to do something about my education. I was still adolescent. I went to every bookshop in town.

With a newly bought volume of Yeats's poems as my passport I went one evening to a meeting I had seen advertised at which someone called Nettie Palmer was to lecture on the Irish Literary Renaissance. During the discussion afterwards I caused quite a stir by speaking of my father's reminiscences of Yeats, A. E., Joyce, Lady Gregory and others connected with the Abbey Theatre. Nettie smiled on learning my name. She had known Gibson before he went abroad and heard he'd brought home an Irish wife but been unable to find him since his return. She was overjoyed to meet me. She took my address and within a week I received a card from her suggesting I should meet her husband for tea at a restaurant in Collins Street. She hoped the description she'd given Vance of me would be enough for him to recognize me. It was. As soon as I went through the door a handsome, suntanned man rose from a seat behind a table in the window.

'Edith Young?' he said, placing a chair opposite his. He was very reserved. He began by asking me how long I'd been in Australia. Getting on for two years, and I still felt a complete stranger.

'Your landscape,' I complained, 'is monotonous. The people are mostly provincial and dull. They're hospitable, kind, and all that, but . . .'

'Take it easy,' he rebuked, smiling. 'Bide your time. Your nostalgia for the old country will begin to wear off. What would you say if I condemned the whole of England from what I had seen of it in the outskirts of London?'

Though born in Australia, even now he didn't know the country. Before the war he'd travelled in Russia. There was a great similarity between Russia and Australia. The untracked forest there had reminded him of the virgin bush.

No, he hadn't been as far south as Rostov, but he'd visited Tolstoy's estate at Yasnya Polyana. The grand old man had shown a lively interest in what he had told him through an interpreter about Australia, its people and its writers. The picture that remained in his mind was that of Tolstoy seated with his back to a window and of birch trees in a snow-laden sky.

'I don't want to be rude,' I said, 'but do you make a living by writing? Your wife said you are a novelist and a literary critic.'

'I do manage,' he said in his slow drawl, 'to sell what I write. Nettie does too. We bring up our two girls on our combined efforts without much difficulty. Now that the wattle's in bloom you must come and see us in our shack at Emerald in the Dandenongs.'

Vance had a way of flattering people by listening to what they had to say as though it were of the utmost importance. So I talked as though a spring inside me was trying to unwind. Soon he knew about my home background, about Gibson's initial struggle to make a living, his parents, the diversity of his interests, of his effort to work up his string quartet so that he might tour the country. Vance advised me to go with him. It would provide an opportunity of seeing more of Australia. But first I must fix a date for a visit to Emerald. 'Persuade your husband', he said 'to take a weekend off and bring your son. My elder daughter will enjoy having a boy about to boss and my younger a playmate.'

I felt almost as carefree on setting out to visit the Palmers with Michael as I had when I set out on my own to pay a visit to my aunt in Cheshire. Getting out on to the platform at Emerald which jutted out like a painted raft into the encroaching tide of open country was as exhilarating as getting out on the platform at Congleton.

The dusty, unpaved and straggling main street of the little township with its weatherboard, colonial-looking hotel, its general store and its Post Office was like a town in a Western. When Vance came cantering down the street on a bay mare to rein up in front of a group of sunburnt men lounging on the veranda of the hotel he could have been the sheriff. Dismounting, he apologized for not being on time, hoisted Michael and the suitcase on to the horse, took the reins, and set off at walking pace, me by his side, down a track through the bush. Gums reared up to a cloudless sky. Tree ferns grew as high as your head. The mocking call of a kookaburra followed us to the brow of a hill and then below us a cascade of wattle washed the gully with gold.

'Is it to shame me for my hasty judgment of your landscape you've invited me to Emerald?' I enquired of Vance.

'Have you begun to see colour in the bush?' he asked, twinkling at me under the shade of his digger's hat.

The Palmers' house squatting in the midst of a sunny paddock encircled by gums was like an island in a sea of encroaching bush.

Michael was off after breakfast to explore with the Palmers' two daughters and seldom appeared except for meals. In the evening we parents gathered in a lamplit room around a fire of glowing logs. Nettie was busy with a pile of darning and I was seated on the hearth at Vance's feet as ready as any schoolgirl with a crush on her teacher for every word that came from his lips. I took his assessment of Australian writers, of whom I knew nothing, to be gospel. He advised me to read Henry Handel Richardson's *Fortunes of Richard Mahoney* as an introduction to Australian literature. His rendering of Shakespeare's *Phoenix and the Turtle* seemed to me superb. The richness of his voice made that strange poem sound like a requiem for all earthly love. It took an Australian to introduce me to this unknown side of Shakespeare.

One afternoon Vance and I set off on Nettie's suggestion to track across country to a timbered shanty clothed in vines belonging to the dramatist, Louis Essen, and his wife. Hilda Essen, a tall, handsome woman who came to welcome us at the gate, reminded me of Ibsen's Hedda Gabler; I could imagine vine leaves in her hair. Louis Essen, a wispy, wizened little man, with an impish smile, a striking contrast to his wife, showed us into a small shuttered room musty with the smell of old books lining its walls. Taking from the shelves his facsimile first editions of Elizabethan dramatists, and blowing dust from the covers, he caressed each as he showed them to us, as he did the newly acquired printing press on which his wife had begun setting the type for his latest one-act play. At tea he railed in his high-pitched cockney twang against the tendency prevalent amongst so many

Australians to believe that the only good writing came from Europe, and in particular from Britain.

'So long as we are dominated by a tradition foreign to our soil,' he complained, 'we shall fail to have a literature of our own. The influence of the ballad mongers, such as Lawson and Paterson, is preferable to importing into our verse the paraphernalia of the English countryside. The Americans have paved the way. It is up to us to follow.' I listened drowsily to him and Vance talking about Australia. They thought all articulate Australians should contribute to a culture that would be indigenous, its roots in the soil.

One thing that surprised me was that the group of Melbourne writers and intellectuals I was later to meet through the Palmers, though marvellously free of both money snobbery and the class distinctions I had become accustomed to at home, seemed to take for granted that the aborigines — the real natives of Australia — should be treated as almost a subhuman, inferior race, impossible to educate other than in the elementary laws of hygiene. The general view was that the Blacks were only fit to be herded into government reserves or relegated to forced labour in the back blocks, preferably in the Northern Territory where the climate was tough. Once when I protested I was told that I didn't know what I was talking about. It was useless to point to the success of the Chinese as market gardeners in and around Melbourne, or say that with more of them and more water the desert interior could blossom like a rose. The 'Chinks', I was told, breed like rabbits. Within a generation there would be a racial problem in Australia, equal to America's. The White Australian policy was a must.

I soon discovered that the Australian showed his emotions in public even less than the English. He had grown a thick skin. He defended himself, by joking, from prying glances and probing questions. I learnt to stick to the general and avoid the particular, to keep away from personal relationships and above all sex. So strictly did I keep to the rules that I was very soon accepted by these Australians as one of themselves.

Once a week I went to a meeting of a literary society held in a room at the back of a secondhand bookshop I believe to have been in an arcade off Collins Street. The proprietor, Ellis Bird, a charming, elderly man presided over the meetings with a courteous eighteenth-century air. It was the common aim of that small group of writers to lift Australia from a colonial status to one of a national identity, to give Australia a voice peculiarly its own in the world of letters. The veteran poet, Bernard O'Dowd, was always the most eloquent. He put lesser poets such as Fernly Mourice and Fred Macarthney in the shade. Vance and Nettie Palmer were the twin deities. I was thrilled when Vance came into the room. I considered Nettie infinitely superior to myself intellectually.

Though privately I questioned the wisdom of Australian novelists or playwrights stressing so much the effect of the local environment on character, rather than revealing character in the light of psychological conflict, I dared not say so. The psychological alienation from reality which is so brilliantly represented in many of the characters in Patrick White's novels seems to me in retrospect to be due to a dichotomy of mind and body I only dimly sensed in many Australian acquaintances, a dichotomy much too difficult for me to probe without causing myself anxiety.

When Vance, who had heard me read some of Yeat's poems, asked me to recite O'Dowd's long descriptive poem *The Bush* at a public meeting I was very excited. On a hot December night, sweating in an evening dress of lime yellow silk, I received as much applause as I had as a child from the audience over which Katherine Tingley presided on White Lotus Day.

As a result I was invited by Vance, Louis Essen and one or two other would-be dramatists to join a dramatic society whose purpose was to introduce to a select (the disguise word for small) Australian audience plays which had literary rather than box office value. I was flattered to have been chosen by a former member of the Abbey Theatre Company who was to produce to take the lead in a bill of Irish one-act plays and I asked Gibson if he'd agree. It would mean being out two or three nights a week at rehearsal. Who would stay at home with Michael? Gibson was as generous as usual. Unless he had to report on a concert, he would. I mustn't miss such an opportunity of using my acting talent.

My star part was that of the old woman in Synge's *Riders to the Sea*. So much did I identify myself with the sorrow of a mother robbed of her five fine sons by a relentless sea that in delivering her lament over the death of her last remaining son, his body washed ashore on the white rocks off the coast of Connemara, I choked with genuine tears and brought the house down.

Fritz Hart, Director of the Conservatorium of Music founded by Nellie Melba, saw my performance and asked me to take his students for voice production and drama.

'Perhaps you can get rid of their Cockney twang,' he said. 'It is laziness as much as the dry climate which makes them slur their vowels.'

Though Gibson did his best to be at home on the nights I was out at rehearsal, if he had to attend a concert Michael suffered more than either of us realized by being left alone in the flat. He seemed fairly resigned when I had told him his bedside story and left him surrounded by his toys and picture books. But he evidently suffered a lot over it. On returning one evening later than usual I found him wide awake on the sleeping-out veranda frantically counting aloud to himself.

'Why aren't you asleep, darling?' I enquired in self-reproach as I tucked in the bedclothes.

'I can't,' he confessed, 'till you come back. I never do. I count, and go on counting, sometimes up to a million and when I've counted a million I tell myself you'll be back. Tonight I had to start all over again.'

This upset me so much that I resolved to give up my ambition to become an actress at his expense, and keep to teaching. My classes at the Conservatorium started me off. Within a year of meeting Fritz Hart I not only had so many private pupils that I had to rent a room in town to teach them in but was appointed as teacher of voice production and drama at several girls' high schools both in Melbourne and the surrounding districts for the daughters of wealthy squatters and businessmen. I was soon earning practically as much as Gibson. We pooled our money to employ a kindly housekeeper to take care of Michael, do the cooking and leave me free.

Gibson had his set of friends; I, mine. We seldom met except at breakfast. So as to see the sunrise over distant ranges and to lie beneath the sky and see the stars at night I moved my bed beside Michael's on to the sleeping-out veranda and left the bedroom to Gibson. We rarely made love any more. When we did it was no good.

We were unfaithful and frank with each other about it. Gibson teased me about a young violinist who deputized for him in his quartet, and I him about his attractive star pupil who was the cellist. I did not tell him that whenever the mild blue eyes of the lean, lanky violinist met mine during a rehearsal the sudden blaze I detected in them fired me too with desire. Gibson knew and was pleased that I had an admirer in Fritz Hart and taunted me for the awe I felt for Vance Palmer; he had no idea how important the violinist had become. The understanding between us was such that he knew what I was going to say before I said it. I introduced him to Nietzsche, he lent me Plato's *Dialogues*. To emulate him I became a vegetarian. One moonlight night I lay with him on the parched grass at Sassafras in the foothills of the Dandenongs. In the shadowy bush I feasted my body on his. I thought afterwards that I was pregnant, but I wasn't.

Then Gibson gave me another shock. On the strength of a letter of introduction to Lord Beaverbrook from a visiting journalist he told me that he had decided to leave Melbourne for a second time to test himself out in London. Mercurial as ever, he believed he could make good. Nothing I said could dissuade him. He was as ready to go back as he'd been to set sail for Australia. His decision swept me back into his arms. I decided to follow him back. As soon as I heard from Gibson that he had found a flat for us in London, I took my by now quite large savings from the bank, paid our passages home, and left an assured living behind me. It was all like my father again setting back home from New York. But this time Lord Beaverbrook was not quite a George Westinghouse.

11 Earls Court

For the first few months after my return London seemed to an exile from the sun to be a brick wilderness. Gibson had rented a flat in Notting Hill Gate. The people in the street, in the shops, on buses seemed to have been paralysed by the General Strike. Hunger marchers tramped the streets. The sky was too low after Australia. Gibson was still on the hunt for the job as musical critic he was after. Though choked by asthma he followed the trail of any influential journalist in Fleet Street who could introduce him to the Editor of the *Express*. In the meantime we lived on the savings I'd brought with me from Australia.

The economic setbacks had not affected my father. He had left White Lodge and now lived in a modern flat overlooking the Thames at the corner of Tite Street in Chelsea. I first called upon my mother on a gloomy November afternoon. A gilded lift took me to the top storey. Mother was plumper and more prosperous looking.

'You're as brown as a native, you've caught the sun.' I said I had, but not, sadly, for keeps.

'Sadly? It's just as well. It doesn't suit you. In that old mac and scarlet scarf you're wearing you look no better than a gypsy. What's good enough for the Australian bush won't do for London. Only well-to-do people live in these flats. The Commissionaire will wonder who you are.'

'Take me as I am, or not at all,' I blazed at her, making for the door just as I'd done before the marriage to Gibson.

'Come now, don't be so quick to take offence. Surely a mother's the right to say what she thinks to her own daughter — for her own good? So that she may make a good impression?'

'On a lift attendant? Mother, for shame.'

'You haven't changed a bit. Just as hot-headed and difficult as ever.'

On the mantelpiece (perhaps got out for the occasion) was a flattering photograph of myself with Michael looking like the angel his namesake which I'd sent her from Melbourne. Had I turned up on her doorstep looking as well groomed as the young woman in the photo I would have received a very different welcome.

She crackled away at me as usual. Gibson couldn't have chosen a worse time to return to London. Such a pity he'd left Australia. Hadn't he known that the country was suffering from economic depression? Supporting myself teaching in Melbourne, it was stupid to have risked joining Gibson until I knew he was earning enough to keep me.

'Don't worry, Mother,' I said, glaring at her. 'I've not come begging. I've never asked you or Father for a penny and hope I never shall.'

'You make me afraid to open my mouth. Gibson's got his father, luckily. As for Daniel he spends all the money he's got and more on the Anthroposophical Society.'

I smiled at the jaw-breaker. What Society did she say? She launched out on my father's devotion to Rudolph Steiner. A former member of the Theosophical Society like himself, he was the founder of Anthroposophy. It was related to theosophy but differed in being concerned, as the name showed, with the wisdom of man rather than god. My father thought Anthroposophy more suitable than Theosophy to modern times. He had first met Dr Steiner in Austria, and had been so impressed by what he thought of as his scientific attitude to occult teaching that he decided to join up with him and he became a founder of the Anthroposophical Society of Great Britain. Since then he had been regularly to conferences at Steiner's headquarters at Dornoch in Switzerland. Anthroposophy went wider than theosophy. Dr Steiner advocated the use of vegetable compost in agriculture in the place of artificial manures and had a theory of medicine derived from homoeopathy. He wanted improvements in education, especially for mentally defective and backward children. He had applied Goethe's theory of colour to painting and developed a style of architecture incorporating forms from nature. He had revived poetic drama, in particular Eurythmy, a type of dance movement like that practised in ancient Greece. My father had sent my sister to Dornoch to study

under Frau Steiner. It was gratifying to him, she told me, to have
a daughter who seemed enthusiastic about his Anthroposophical
work. Aileen had a talent as a dancer which might well make her
one of Frau Steiner's star pupils.

I listened abstractedly. Her eyes as she went on became more
and more dreamy. The tugboats hooted outside on the river.

' "By their fruits ye shall know them".' I quoted to try and
puncture her a bit. 'How do anthroposophists behave? Action is
the test of faith.'

'Dr Steiner practises what he preaches, even if the members of
the Society don't. They're good, bad and indifferent, like everyone
else. Some I like, others I don't.'

'I take it you've jumped on with father?'

She said that unless she shared his interests she might as well
be widowed or divorced. She saw precious little of him anyway.
Since he was appointed General Secretary of the British Society,
he was not only out at meetings most nights of the week, but had
given more than he could reasonably afford (but what about the
gilded lift then?) to the fund he was raising for a hall in Baker
Street large enough for a lecture room and theatre for performances of Eurythmy and Dr Steiner's liturgical plays. The Rudolph
Steiner Hall was to be mainly for the Society but could be hired by
others for public performances. It was a venture my father had set
his heart on, so she couldn't complain.

She spoke with resignation. I told her I envied her the view of
the river. 'It keeps me from being lonely,' she said.

Recognizing regret for days past in her voice, I kissed her
goodbye. But when to prevent her ringing for the lift attendant
I walked down the many flights of stairs I realized it had been
very odd she had not suggested I should bring her grandson
Michael to see her. Remembering how blessed I'd been in the love
of *my* grandmother, to pay mother out I determined not to call
at Tite Street again unless I was asked to bring my son.

The heart of London was the studio my brother now had at
Wimbledon on the Ridgeway within easy walking distance of
White Lodge. Partly to be a bit nearer it we left the expensive
flat at Notting Hill Gate for a roomy attic in a gloomy, late
Georgian House in the Earls Court Road. Even though it was only
one room I much preferred the white-washed attic and the view
over roof tops from its dormer window to our former flat. A new
room with a view always raised my spirits for a bit. The house

belonged to an Italian woman, a widow, who'd known my father in his theosophical days and who said she was therefore prepared to let the attic to his daughter for a modest pound a week. She also kindly let us have a double divan, the worse for wear, and lent us a camp bed for Michael to put in the part of the attic which did for a kitchen.

On Saturdays I took Michael to Wimbledon to spend the afternoon with his cousin Joan, Ronald and Flora's pretty little daughter who was a year younger. Joan was full of mischief. Flora and I had whispered soul talks in the studio. Students and my brother's artistic hangers-on were always around painting each other in shirts, overalls, with and without hats. My brother was going through what he termed his 'dynamic' period. This meant, I gathered, that he concentrated only on that bit of his subject which interested him and made that the centre of the composition, only sketching in the rest lightly. Exaggerated highlights in one part of the canvas accentuated depths of shadow in another. The method produced an effect often strikingly dramatic. At a break for tea, the group discussed each other's work with complete frankness which developed into an argument which Ronald dominated.

At the private view of an exhibition in a small West End Gallery at which some of Ronald's landscapes were shown he introduced me to one of his artist friends. He made a strong impression on me. I arrived late and unable to see anyone I knew in the chattering crowd I made straight for Ronald and tugged at his arm.

'Who's your girl friend?' enquired a shabbily dressed fellow with a panama hat stuck like a casque of Hermes on the back of his dark hair.

'Meet my sister, Mark,' Ronald said. 'Mrs Gibson Young, recently returned from Australia to join her husband in London. She looks a colonial, doesn't she?'

'Looks fine to me,' he responded gallantly.

My brother wearing the uniform of his calling — beard, flowing tie, black felt hat — spotted a possible buyer and went off. I was overcome by shyness.

'Your brother has come on in the art world since you left home,' said my companion, offering me a cigarette. His fingers I noticed, as he gave me a light, were stained with ink, his frayed shirt cuffs smudged with paint.

'He has. And you, I see by your cuffs are also a painter.'

'Trust a woman to spot it. I paint in my spare time, to please myself. For a living I do commercial art. Disappointed?'

'No. Why?'

'Oh yes, you are, starry eyes. It would be your romantic idea of artists that I should starve in a garret rather than prostitute my art for commercial purposes.'

He said that the whole bloody art world was a racket. Fashions in painting changed as quickly as fashions in clothes. The dealers got most of the money there was for it. Dealers, private patrons, artists were all rocking about together in the same leaky boat.

'But I expect you're convinced that art should be practised for art's sake alone, and that I'm talking through my hat. Or lack talent.'

At this point Flora came sailing towards us. She told us proudly that Ronald had sold his large canvas of the boats for forty pounds to the owner of the gallery for his permanent collection.

'Should have made it double for that shark,' growled my companion. 'I bet the frame cost a fiver.'

'But Ronnie Clark didn't take a commission.' Flora said. 'He must believe Ronald has a future or he wouldn't have bought it. Ronald's delighted.'

'I'm sure he is. Congratulate him for me. Oh, look, there's old Archie.'

Waving a catalogue at a man in a bowler who'd just entered the gallery he left us abruptly to make his way through the crowd.

I could not at once account for my sense of loss as I watched him, holding himself like a drill-sergeant, wedge his way through the people. Then suddenly it occurred to me that he reminded me of Grisha. Not in appearance — he was not good-looking like Grisha but in the aggressive, hammering way he talked. I asked Flora if he were a communist.

Not to her knowledge. Though he was working-class in origin she didn't believe he had any political affiliations. He was just an artist. His life had been one perpetual struggle. He lived in a small room above his aunt's sweet shop in South Wimbledon. It was all he had. His mother died at an early age from cancer. His father had neglected him and his aunt had reared him as best she could on her small income. In return he had to help her in the shop and deliver papers before and after school. He'd shown a talent for drawing at school which had got him a grant to the Royal College of Art. Ronald believed that if he'd not continually criticized the teaching methods of his tutors at the college and left, disgruntled, half way through the course he might well have won the Rome Scholarship. He blamed class distinction amongst the students at the college for making it impossible for him. He had spoilt what might well have been a successful career as a painter.

Ronald admired him enough to invite him to use his studio whenever he felt inclined. He found Mark Parry a stimulus and a challenge.

'Mark needs sympathetic understanding,' Flora continued. 'He gets people's backs up.'

'He's certainly an odd fellow — as different from Ronald as Cain from Abel. Brother enemies — that's what they are.'

'I hadn't thought of them like that,' she said. 'It's right though.'

12 Monkey Island

For a bottle party at the studio on Christmas Eve Flora invited the three of us to Wimbledon — Michael to share Joan's room at her parents' flat across the road, Gibson and myself to sleep on a mattress on the studio floor. The party was in full swing when I got there. Candles were stuck in beer bottles. Couples rotated in an atmosphere blue with smoke to a waltz tune churned out by a wheezy gramophone. Ronald wasn't dancing. He was at the back of the studio loudly expounding his theories of painting to a group of admirers. Flora, high up on a cushioned couch was talking earnestly to an aesthetic looking young man leaning attentively over her bared shoulder.

A couple of young men, Mark one of them, were helping themselves to drink at an improvised bar behind a corner screen. I was lingering by the door uncertain what to do when Mark, elbowing through the dancers, grasped me by the waist and whirled me away. He crushed me to his breast, and with a rapturous smile rested his cheek on my hair. When the dance was over he covered my mouth with a breath-taking kiss.

'That's the stuff,' he said with relish. 'I've been thirsty for that kiss ever since I met you at the Gallery. It took booze to give me the courage.'

'Your breath stinks of beer,' I said, struggling to free myself from his grasp. 'Taking by storm doesn't go down well with me.'

'Oh no you don't. You can't get away as easily as all that. Look into my eyes.' Clasping my chin, he tilted my face up to his. 'You have lovely eyes, as blue and distant as the sky, not altogether human, nor as innocent as they seem to be.'

'You can't see them properly by candle-light. They're grey like yours.' He shook his head. He couldn't allow that. His were green and mine were blue to match my hair.

'Sunshine and blue skies,' he declared, 'are just what I need.'

His smile began to take effect on me. I didn't pull away after all. I accused him of being a romantic. 'You're right,' he agreed. 'Where women are concerned I'm a hopeless romantic.'

'A dose of the clap,' he said, linking my arm and leading me to the bar, 'would cure me of that nonsense. A woman like you could twist me round her little finger. That is,' he added, as he poured me out a glass of burgundy, 'if I let her.'

I thought it odd he should use exactly the same expression as Gibson had used, the night he had crept into my bedroom at White Lodge, and carrying me to the mirror like the Swedish girl had ordered me to inspect my body. To drown my uneasy feeling I drank the wine at one go. He refilled my glass and as I had eaten nothing the wine went to my head. I was deliciously and recklessly drunk. Feeling friendly to everyone I glanced again around the studio. The candle-light was kind to Flora. She looked scarcely a day older than when I left her in the hall of the villa in Hale eight or more years before. Ronald had become almost as fine a figure of a man as his Scottish grandfather in his prime. The bumps on his forehead going back to that evil day in New York when I had imagined him dead in the janitor's arms were now characteristics which indicated a talent for painting.

Stroking his beard he was smiling blandly at a dark, animated girl with the look of a Spanish gypsy in her eye. Slipping an arm round her slim waist he stopped talking and started dancing. Slowly, tipsily, they swayed together.

'Ronald seems sweet on that girl,' I said to Mark. 'Who is she?'

'Flora's headache,' he replied, grinning. 'You know Flora. She believes every girl her beloved husband takes a fancy to is a threat; but as she has it firmly fixed in her mind that it is her duty to allow him freedom to express himself she suffers in silence while old R.O.D. enjoys himself.'

'But there's no real danger is there?' I asked anxiously.

'Don't worry, sister. Their marriage may show signs of wearing thin, but I daresay it can easily be patched up. What about your own? How threadbare is that?' he enquired.

'We've been married ten years and still going strong.'

'Congratulations,' he said, thumping me on the back.

Infected by the couples kissing in corners, the clatter, laughter, thud of feet and the wine, I whirled in a solo dance, my hair down my back, chanting: 'It's love, it's love that makes the world go round.'

Mark grasped my arm. 'Steady now. Sober up. Your husband has just arrived.'

'So what?' I said, flicking a hand across his cheek. 'You're the last one to tell me to behave.'

Gibson produced a bottle of whisky from his coat pocket and offered it to Flora, with apologies for being late, as a contribution to a party that was fast fizzling out.

Waking from a restless sleep on the mattress on which I'd tossed at Gibson's side to a grey, cold dawn I saw Mark lying on the hearth, bundled in his overcoat, close to the popping gas fire. Why did he upset me? Physically, there was nothing particularly attractive about him. Short, dark, stocky, with a tousled mop of hair falling over his collar, his blunt features were only redeemed by a generous smile.

I had not had time to forget him when he turned up on our doorstep. He came ahead of the landlady up the stairs and without knocking entered the attic. I was startled. I was washing up the breakfast things in a bowl on the kitchen table. What happened seemed again to be inevitable. The yearning in his eyes drove me into his arms. Our hands trembled. His were as cold as ice.

'You're shivering. What's wrong?'

'I'm in love,' he said huskily. 'And I don't know what to do about it.'

'There's never anything to be done,' I told him gravely.

'There must be. Something must be done.' He kissed me lingeringly.

'One thing is certain,' I said, laughing hysterically. 'You can't come here making love to me.'

'It's equally certain that I must make love to you. I don't mind where, when and how. It's just got to be.'

'You're mad,' I scolded, 'crazy.'

'Sure I'm crazy.' Whirling me along he would have had me on the camp bed in an instant if I'd not stubbornly resisted him.

'O.K.,' he said with a shrug. 'Have it your own way. I can wait. What about a nice cup of tea?'

As I busied myself with this he paced up and down puffing smoke rings with his eyes fixed on me.

'I have decided,' he announced, 'that I must paint you, seated as you are now at the table, with the blue wall as background. Promise me you'll fix it up with your husband and give me a date. Your attic could do with a fresh coat of whitewash. I'll do that as part of the bargain. If your landlady takes me for a house decorator that's all to the good.'

With a 'cheerio' he clattered downstairs.

My relationship with Gibson had got so much worse since my return from Australia that I had an excuse for listening to my heart. Money troubles were partly to blame. We were hard pushed to find the rent or money for food. My savings were down to a meagre five pounds. I resented his spending my money on treating his journalist friends to drinks. He complained I was everlastingly grumbling at him for his extravagance, and always of my continued sexual frigidity. When he lost his temper with me I treated him with a cold disdain which I knew infuriated him still further.

So I encouraged Mark to come once a week ostensibly to paint my portrait. I was his first love. In that lay its enchantment, for a woman ten years older than him who imagined that her sex life had died too early a death. He made me feel young again. As he sat at the kitchen table relaxing after a brief spell of concentration on a painting which we both knew was merely an excuse, I felt powerfully, voluptuously, physically drawn to him. In fact the more I saw of him, the stronger and more irresistible it became.

Gibson at first treated him with a tolerance similar to that with which he'd once treated Grisha.

'This room stinks of turps and smoke,' he would say, sniffing in disgust. 'It makes me cough. He's taking a hell of a time over his portrait. He's done quite a good likeness of the teapot.'

'It's not supposed to be a portrait. It's a painting. He's as much interested in the teapot as in me,' I said lamely.

'Why not paint his own teapot? You'd better mind your step, my girl, or you'll be losing your husband. Have you seen who's taken the attic across the landing?'

'No, but I see you have. Madame Meducci told me she's letting the attic to Gordon Craig's daughter-in-law.'

'In-law? Married, is she? That's a blow. I carried up her bags for her yesterday and was bowled over. She has the arrogance of a Borgia and the face of a virgin—an exotic mixture that's enough to go to any man's head.'

'I understand she's separated from her husband. So now's your chance. Go ahead, cultivate her acquaintance. History always repeats itself.'

'Ah, maybe,' he said, a glint in his eye. 'But with just that little difference which makes all the difference in the world. What I did in the past to save our marriage I can't do again. I can't again call upon my father.'

'Is that a warning?'

'Take it as you please.'

Elsa Craig's beauty bewitched me as much as it had Gibson. I met her on the stairs going up to the attic. She responded to my friendly smile with the impassive, lifeless stare of a statue. To my 'good morning' she inclined her head; and as from the landing I watched her graceful descent I noticed that her dress showed off the sweeping curve of her back, her slim hips and thighs. From a bodice fastened up to the neck and moulded to her figure so as to show off her breasts, a skirt flowed in statuesque folds to her ankles. Her colours were startling: scarlet, gentian blue, mustard yellow, or black, each in turn a striking contrast to the magnolia pallor of her complexion and her heavy ashblond hair. Her eyes were deepset above prominent cheek bones. Their inhumanity was that of a moon creature. This woman who attracted in turn I don't know how many men, including my husband and Jack Lindsay, the Australian author, who writes about her as his wife in that portion of his autobiography entitled *Fanfrolico and After*, captured my imagination to such an extent that I made her the heroine of my novel, *Lisa*, published by Dent in the early thirties and later in America. She became in my novel a symbol of the legendary woman whom all men seek but whom none may possess.

On looking back to that period of my marriage, marked by recriminations culminating in partial reconciliations for the sake of our son, it seems to me that Gibson in delivering his ultimatum was as keen to end it as I was. He certainly made it perfectly clear that unless I gave up seeing Mark he would leave me.

'Make up your mind,' he demanded, 'which means most to you. Either him or me. According to your choice, so I make my plans. I am no more willing to share you with him than I was to share you with that fellow, Fichzon.'

'Have you forgotten what effect a separation is likely to have on Michael?'

I felt as I had before over Grisha. I seemed to have no will of my own, but drifted from one state of mind to another, like a cork thrown about on a tide. I also developed claustrophobia. I felt literally choked. Even in a bus I came out in cold sweats, suffered palpitations and was obliged to cling to the seat to stop myself yielding to an overwhelming temptation to fling myself on the floor in a faint. I had similar symptoms each time I went with Gibson to a concert. Rather than make an exhibition of myself in the hall I spent most of the evening in the foyer or the lavatory. To take the Underground to Wimbledon was out of the question. Since the talk with Gibson I had forbidden Mark to come to the house. But I used to meet him for tea in a workers' café in the Earls Court Road. He refused at first to take Gibson's threat seriously. He was only trying me on to see how far he could act the possessive husband. But when he realized how upset I was he changed his line.

'Cheer up, sweetheart,' he coaxed. 'There's nothing your old Mark wants more than to have you to himself—for keeps. Trust yourself to him. He won't let you down. The trouble is you don't know what you want. If you did, I'd take as a studio that large room Madame Meducci has to let on the ground floor and there's not a thing Gibson could do about it.'

'Except divorce me.'

'I doubt he'd be so obliging. Not that is unless he intends to replace you by Elsa.'

I pleaded with him not to do anything rash and he agreed to wait until Gibson and I had sorted things out.

The depression over our household not only led Gibson to spend most of his free evenings in Elsa's company but affected Michael as it had when he was a baby. He recognized that all was not well between us. Whenever I saw him gravely watching me as I did the housework or prepared his meals I tried to make myself appear cheerful. He was not deceived. While trying to make up my mind I repeatedly asked myself what I wanted from Mark that was worthwhile making my son unhappy for, and found mainly a longing to be with him. When I recalled his harsh voice, his Cockney accent, his laughter, the gaiety of his smile, I felt that only through him could I discover an undiscovered part of myself that had never grown. Without him I would shrink into an obedient and frigid wife. To prevent this should I not risk a hazardous life with a penniless artist?

When I passed on the result of these heart-searchings to Gibson he surprised me by saying with melancholy resignation that if I really felt as I described it was perhaps right that we should part, temporarily at any rate. As we might want to come together again he wouldn't consider divorce.

'To explain it to Michael is quite beyond me,' he confessed. 'As his mother you should do it.'

'First we must agree to share him equally. I will not be deprived of him.'

'Naturally. Anything else would be as intolerable for me as it would for you. The boy means more to me than anyone else in the world.'

I broached it to Michael by asking him if he'd noticed (as I knew he had) how miserable I had been lately. He had, and wanted to know why. As abject as a criminal, I confessed that his father and I had been so unhappy together since I returned from Australia that we had decided to part.

'You mean,' he said in a tone of withering reproach, 'that you and Daddy are no longer going to be together?'

Nodding, I implored him with tears in my eyes not to fret. Said that whatever happened I would never leave him; that Gibson loved him as much as I did, and that neither of us would ever agree to anything that would prevent him sharing our lives.

'Don't cry, Mimi,' he said, slipping a hand to the back of my neck, as had been his habit when he saw me distressed. 'If you are unhappy together, I suppose it's better to part. But it does seem rather silly to me.'

His apparent stoicism set a good example for me.

Once we had decided, Gibson again appealed to his father to help with Michael's education. He agreed to pay the fees of a boarding school at Bristol recommended to Gibson by a fellow Australian. When we went together to inspect the school we were deceived into believing that the Headmaster and his wife were an enlightened, kindly couple. We hardly felt any compunction in sending Michael there at the beginning of the spring term.

When Gibson left for a flat in Shepherds Market and persuaded Elsa Craig to join him there, he had at last got the job as musical critic to the *Daily Express* he'd been trying to get for so long. Mark moved into the part-furnished ground floor room at Madame Meducci's. To provide Michael with a neutral ground on which we could be together in the holidays I kept on the attic at Gibson's expense until such time as I was able to afford something else.

Mark set a light to my smouldering sex. When I blamed myself for seeking my happiness at the expense of my son's, Mark would shut my lips with a kiss and say: 'We've only one life. Let's make the most of it.'

His room had a sombre grandeur. A chair proudly described by Madame as genuine Chippendale waited, like a gentleman in an ante-chamber, by the door which he'd taken the liberty of painting lion-yellow. There was a trestle table at which he worked on his commercial designs: and in a cupboard carved and embossed in gilt he stuffed his few poor clothes and his paints. A silvery aspen tree filled a bay window over a divan on which we made love by day and at night.

The trembling of his limbs opened my mouth to receive his tongue. His moist lips quiveringly withdrew their pressure only to renew their thrust. The rhythmic play of his hands fondling my breasts made it as easy for me to achieve an orgasm as for him.

So that I might see the leaves of the aspen tossed by the wind I asked him not to close the shutters at night. On the creaking divan I made up a poem:

> The dark cold earth
> Under fields of snow
> Holds fire for seed.
>
> In dark warm bed
> Under sheets of snow
> A woman sleeps with her man.
>
> 'Stay,' pleads he, 'the night is long,
> Soft, my love, and slow.'
> 'The night,' says she, 'is short, my love,
> The reign of death is long.
>
> Press close, my love.
> Your hair is meadowsweet.
> All flesh grass.'

Rocking me to and fro in his arms he would say: 'I lose myself in your eyes . . .'

My father wrote to say that he'd heard that Gibson and I had separated and would I come to discuss it at lunch in town—as though it was for a business appointment. I met him outside his office in Kingsway. Muffled in overcoat and scarf on a warm spring day he hailed a passing taxi and handing me in gently as though I were his girl gave the driver an address of a smart restaurant in Mayfair. I told him about what had gone wrong between me and Gibson, but was afraid to mention Mark. He listened abstractedly and raising his eyes from his dish of grilled sole remarked casually that a marriage such as ours was doomed to failure. Though it was hard on Michael, the best thing we could have done in the circumstances was to send him to a boarding school.

'You don't blame me, father?' I stuttered nervously.

'Blame you? For what? For refusing to commit adultery? In my opinion, to live with a man you have ceased to love is adultery. But see you don't make the same mistake again,' he warned. 'Once bitten twice shy. Until you give Gibson cause for divorce it is his duty to keep you. Legally he is still responsible for you. You must make that clear to him.'

'But if I'm giving him nothing—and I'm not—why should he be expected to keep me?' I objected. 'He has promised to be financially responsible for Michael. That's all I want.'

He looked uneasy and the distance between us was more than the width of the table.

'If you propose to let him off so lightly,' he said, questioning me with judicial eyes over his pince-nez, 'what do you intend to live on?'

'Teaching dramatic art and literature as I did in Australia. The certificate I hold and the letters of recommendation I have from Melbourne should surely get me work.'

My father was giving his penniless daughter a treat. With the flavour of an English strawberry on my tongue I would not swallow my pride and tell him I had only a few pounds left in the world.

'I'm all right, father. Gibson's paid a couple of months' rent in advance for my room. Something will turn up. If the worse comes to the worst I can always go to a Labour Exchange and take what's offered.'

'Don't do that,' he advised. 'I can let you have five pounds to be going on with and if you'd care to go down to our house near Guildford for a month or two, by all means do. Mother won't be using it much this summer. She is coming with me to an Anthroposophical Conference at the Hague. From there we're going to Dornoch. So if you don't mind little Elsie as housekeeper, you're welcome to use it.'

He also said that if I failed to get a job teaching he would pay for a course for me in shorthand-typing at a secretarial college. A typist could always earn enough to keep herself.

With a five pound note in my purse and a kiss on the lips that was none too paternal I trod lightly on the pavement but when I reached the house and told Mark of what had happened he exploded.

'You hypocrite! Posing to your father as the virtuous, brave, little wife, and leaving me out of it as though I didn't exist! If you hadn't had me all ready, you'd never have had the courage to leave Gibson, and you know it. If you're ashamed of me, I'll clear out.'

'Let's go together to Guildford,' he said a little later. 'Tonight, tomorrow, the day after. I don't care when. Let's spend a honeymoon at your parents' house.' I laughed and said that if he came with me Elsie would tell my parents.

'So what? They'll have to know about me sooner or later, so why not now?'

I gave in. I went first to prepare the way, and he followed a week later. We wandered through meadows hedged by wild roses, buttercups and sweet with new mown hay. Summer created a honeymoon country. Poppies glowed amongst corn. The elms were rich with shade.

As Elsie could not prevent us making use of the neat little suburban house she made the best of it. She seemed to get a vicarious pleasure from watching us kissing. Seated by the French window open to the lawn at the back of the house Elsie sewed and Mark, a sketchbook open on his knee, watched my lips as I read aloud from Chaucer's *Troilus and Cressida*.

To Elsie I was still the Persephone she had known at White Lodge and she suggested I had been snatched into the Kingdom of Darkness by Pluto, the King of the Underworld.

'You complement each other,' she said, blinking at us behind her glasses and purring like an ageing cat. 'I never thought Gibson was right for Edith. He was far too worldly. Persephone belongs to Pluto.' So I nicknamed Mark Plute, short for Pluto.

Going back to Earls Court at the end of a month was a return to reality. To economize I gave up the attic and with Madame's permission shared Plute's room, agreeing to her request to take

his name. It was a bad time to look for work. He worked instead.
He didn't spare himself to get enough money so that I could have
a home for my son when he returned from school at the end of
July. He did. He found a bungalow on Monkey Island on the
Thames near Maidenhead which proved an idyllic holiday home.
Lapped by the river, its windows looked out on pleasure boats,
on grassy banks, perfect for children. Flora came down to stay at
the hotel on the island and brought Joan with her as companion
to Michael.

The children were out all day in all weathers. A waterproof
tent provided by Flora was their wigwam. They picnicked over
a fire of brushwood in the wild part by the river beyond the
round house with a turret which was allegedly the retreat of
George IV after his insanity had prevented him from being in
the public eye. I believe that holiday was the best time of their
young lives. Walnut trees shaded the grass in front of a brick and
weatherboard hotel. When Plute returned in the evening from the
commercial art studio in Holborn he used to take me up the river
in a rowing boat that was moored within a couple of yards of
our bungalow. He had to be at the studio by nine. He got his
own breakfast and brought me a cup of tea in bed before he set
off to ferry himself in a punt to the mainland.

Gibson turned up at weekends to see Michael. He was
beginning to do well for money. As well as music critic he had
started to conduct community singing—something for which he
had a flair. Before long he was conducting at Cup Finals and
once a choir of 100,000 people in Hyde Park. In a Harris tweed
suit and a cap to match he impressed the staff at the hotel as a
country gentleman and he had the head waiter hopping about in
expectation of a handsome tip. Relaxed in a deck chair on the
lawn after one evening meal he confided to Flora within my hearing that he was having trouble with Elsa.

'It's murder. She flies into a range about nothing at all, heaps
insults on me, slanders my friends, Edith included, and what's
more, threatens to commit suicide if I leave her, as I must next
month, to report on Beecham's appearance with the Hallé
Orchestra in Manchester.' When Flora said that in that case
Elsa was obviously unsuited to him and was therefore unhappy, he
retorted that she was temperamentally incapable of being happy
with anyone. He scoffed at Flora's idea that he should bring her
to Monkey Island for a weekend. 'She'd throw herself in the

river to cause a sensation or make me wild by flirting outrageously with Mark.' He never knew what she'd do next. She might well take advantage of his absence to disappear with some other man. She had already captivated Jack Lindsay. But she was the loveliest woman he had ever had the misfortune to meet.

After Gibson came to fetch Michael to take him back to school and Flora had returned to Wimbledon with her daughter I was left alone. The wind began to bluster. The river was suddenly deserted. The hotel subsided into silence. Mist hid the mainland and I, with hours to fill in each day, set to work to map out a number of syllabuses for courses in Dramatic Literature and Play Production which I thought might appeal to the L.C.C. or societies for adult education. I wrote off and as an address I gave my brother's at Wimbledon, asking Flora to forward replies. She wrote by return to warn me that my parents would shortly be moving their country cottage from Guildford to a bungalow on the main road between Monkey Island and the village of Bray. A wealthy anthroposophical friend of my father's intended to hold meetings at her fine old manor house on the river within walking distance of Bray. She had told them I was staying at Monkey Island with Mark until the end of October. My father took the news with his usual tolerance. Mother didn't. 'Tell that pair to keep clear of me,' she warned.

Plute treated the letter which upset me so much as good news. 'Serves you right,' he said. 'You'll now have to introduce me whether you like it or not.'

I assured him I had no intention of going near them unless they first called on me. But one Saturday morning when we were passing the house my mother happened to be standing on the doorstep shaking crumbs from a tablecloth on to the lawn for the birds.

'Now's your chance,' said Plute, shoving me through the gate. Boldly he marched up the garden path, myself in tow, and grinning from ear to ear startled my mother by clamping a hand on her arm.

'As your daughter refuses to introduce me I'll introduce myself,' he said, holding out a hand which she ignored.

The colour flooded her cheeks. Looking him up and down she addressed herself to me.

'You're at liberty to make a mess of your life if you've a mind to, but I won't be a party to it. You must have come to a pretty pass if this impudent young man is the best you can do for yourself.'

'Now, now, Mrs Dunlop,' rebuked Plute good-humouredly. 'All is not gold that glitters. A discerning woman like yourself should not judge by appearance alone. Shake hands, won't you?'

'I'll do no such thing. I refuse to recognize you as Edith's partner. What she sees in you is beyond my understanding. I judge a man's qualities by his tone of voice (she presumably meant by his accent). Yours grates on my nerves terribly.'

'I don't. I judge a woman by how she responds to a kiss.' Seizing her in his arms he attempted to kiss her cheek. She shoved him off. 'None of your impertinence,' she scolded, her eyes blazing.

'I admire your spirit,' he returned with a disarming smile. 'I admire your blue eyes. I'd like fine to have you for a mother-in-law, but . . .' Pausing, he wagged his finger at her, 'As you're too mean to invite us in for a cup of tea I intend to treat your snobbery with the contempt it deserves. We shall not trouble you again. Goodbye.'

Delighted at his parting words, I linked my arm with his and we left her, flabbergasted, staring after us from the doorstep.

We locked the door of the bungalow with a rusted key. Plute went to deliver it to the hotel. I plucked a bunch of sleepy marigolds that had defied the frost which rimmed the nasturtium leaves. An old waiter ferried us to the mainland. Wiping a drop off his nose with a soiled apron he pocketed the tip we could ill afford. We stood on the bank watching him punt back to the island.

13 Chelsea

We had to separate for a time after leaving Monkey Island. We had nowhere to go. Plute went to stay with his aunt at Wimbledon; Flora put me up. Gibson came to our aid. His friend, Philip Heseltine, who under the pseudonym of Peter Warlock was making a name for himself as a composer, wanted to let his studio at Ebury Street, Chelsea, for six months to a reliable tenant. Plute saw it and to stake his claim put together all the money he had in the world to send Peter Warlock a month's rent in advance.

The house consisted of two rooms, one up, one down. A large window faced a dreary block of flats. A mirror in a frame lacquered in Chinese red took up practically the whole of one wall and gave a sense of space to the studio. The furniture was a huge divan and shelves stacked with music scores. The original rose-tinted colour of the walls showed through flakes in the off-white distemper. I liked that very much. Shut away from the world in that little studio our ordinary life together began in earnest.

Using me as a model Plute began painting again. He painted me crouched over a gas fire in a blue frock; in my chemise; emerging, wrapped in a towel, from a hip bath. I don't know what has happened to those paintings since but I remember being so thrilled by the one of myself in the chemise that when Plute insisted on me soaping him in the bath tub I kissed his feet in recognition of his talent, flattery which he disdained by threatening to beat me.

Though he had to keep on the job at the commercial studio he devoted the evenings to his own work. I loved to see him absorbed in painting; and when he set to work to model a head of me in clay it struck me that as his feeling for form was better than his sense of colour he would make a better sculptor than a painter. He scorned the idea. If he could draw naturally he could model. I failed to understand how much sensuous pleasure the pigment gave him. Delighted with the delicate, idealized head he modelled I persuaded him to give it permanence by casting it in plaster and carried it about with me as a kind of talisman to perpetuate my youth for several years.

Gibson was having more trouble with Elsa. He turned up at the studio one evening looking haggard and dejected with bags under his eyes and a tale of woe. His affair had reached a dramatic climax. He wanted our sympathy and we gave it without stint once he'd told us.

He'd accused Elsa of sleeping with Jack Lindsay while he was away in Manchester and she'd then snatched a carving knife from the table and slashed a vein in her wrist. A small fountain of blood spurted from it. She reeled and nearly fell. Alarmed by her pallor he had torn up an old shirt to bandage her wrist, given her a stiff brandy, carried her, half fainting, to the bed and dashed out of the house into a taxi. He told the doctor at the casualty department of the nearest hospital that the wound had been caused by an unfortunate slip of a sharp knife whilst carving a joint. The doctor came back with him. Gibson was very persuasive. She submitted passively to having the wound cleaned and stitched and to an injection to prevent possible infection and with the aid of a sedative had slept peacefully for the remainder of the night.

'The woman's crazy,' remarked Plute, 'she might well have stabbed you with the knife instead of herself.'

Gibson thought there was method in it. She wanted to show that if he prevented her seeing Lindsay she was prepared to do away with herself. He believed she had suicidal tendencies. I said that if she was mentally unbalanced it was foolish to keep her tied to him against her will.

'You're right, I suppose,' he admitted. 'I don't want a repetition of that ghastly night.'

When Gibson turned up again to invite us to dinner with him at an Italian restaurant in Soho his natural ebullience had reasserted itself. Rather than continue to live with a woman who would ultimately drive him as crazy as she was herself, he had agreed to Elsa taking a basement flat in Eaton Square. She would bring Lindsay there. If he stayed it would relieve him of further responsibility. He wished the pair of them luck. He talked animatedly of the charms of a new girl whom he'd met at Curwen's, the music publishers. He was quickly over Elsa.

Though I had heard of Jack Lindsay in Melbourne I did not meet him until he was introduced to Gibson by the wife of P. R. Stephenson, the young man who later collaborated with Lindsay in running his *Fanfrolico Press*. When Gibson was courting Elsa I was surprised to come upon her bidding Lindsay a lingering farewell on the landing outside our rooms. Like a painting by Burne-Jones she had stood silhouetted against the light from the open door, her hand in his. I saw at once by the expression in his childlike eyes that she'd got him.

Shy, and bubbling with energy, he was always flashing out ideas when he called on us at Ebury Street. Unable to follow his interpretation of Blake's Prophetic Books which I didn't know till later, I used to switch to Elsa since I suspected that he was only interested in me in order to learn more about Elsa.

On reading of his painful life with Elsa in his *Fanfrolico and After* I saw that he'd quoted passages from *Lisa* as evidence of my insight into her neurotic character. He did not realize I had endowed her with my own feelings. I didn't know her well enough to understand her.

Plute accused me of being so afraid of losing my precious individuality that I dared not commit myself wholly to him. I could not explain, since I did not then know, that I imagined capitulation would bring rejection. I was, and still am, afraid of my femininity. Not understanding the reasons which prevented me from responding to Plute as a woman I attributed the rift it was causing between us to difference in age. After the first phase was over I often felt as much apart during intercourse as is a seapink in a rock from the surging tide beneath. But if he was preoccupied and distant, I would paradoxically ache with desire for him. If only he had left me alone I might have learnt to be as captive to him as I was in the days when we were first in love.

By the time we had to leave Ebury Street for a furnished flat in Oakley Street, Chelsea, I wanted to include other people more in our lives. This was made easier because the Secretary of the Workers' Educational Association, impressed by the syllabus I'd sent him, invited me to an interview which led to his offering me a course on the History of Drama at Woking. He regarded the course as a test and since he'd promised that if I made a success of it I would be taken on the panel of W.E.A. tutors I *had* to succeed. My knowledge of the origins of Greek drama was one of the things I was hazy about and I spent hours on it in the British Museum. I wrote out my lectures at first. It didn't work. To hold the interest of the people who came to the classes, I had to speak extempore. My acting came in useful. As it turned out, instead of the number of people falling off — as I had been warned by the Secretary would probably happen — by the end of the first term the numbers had increased and the discussions that followed each lecture were very lively. The report from the class secretary was so good that I was offered classes in the same subject elsewhere in the London district. It helped to pass an oral exam in the History of Drama at County Hall. Once I'd been taken on the L.C.C. panel, I was out teaching most evenings of the week; and in six months from the first class at Woking was earning enough, modest as it was, to make me financially independent of Plute.

Sexual conflict was diverted temporarily into politics. The simplification of Marxist principles in John Strachey's *Coming Struggle for Power* convinced me, as it did Plute, that a politically conscious working class was the only protection against Fascism. I began to talk the jargon. The revolt of the intellectuals against outworked bourgeois values even if it was little more than a liberal reform movement gave the lead to a group of young poets and others who became the angry young men of the thirties. They waged war on all types of oppression, political or person. Left Book Club publications multiplied.

In the belief that form should serve the content in painting as much as in the 'proletarian novel' and the theatre Plute took an active part in creating the early Artists' International Association. Reacting against the growing influence of the Surrealist Movement in France on certain members of the A.I.A. he joined the other extreme wing who, in my opinion, wanted to make art into propaganda. I accused him of turning out pictures that were really posters. He accused me of being a petit-bourgeois, liberal, idealist. Although he said he believed in the equality of the sexes and approved of a woman, whether married or single, earning her own living, it didn't seem to work with us. Instead of my independence uniting, it divided us, as it had with Gibson.

But when he grew a beard, that red tuft on his chin made him immensely attractive to me again. I fell in love with him all over again.

I.O.—K

Then he joined instead of just supporting the Communist Party and shaved off his beard and I felt I had lost him. I couldn't be left out. So I too applied for a Party card. I was refused and was told I'd have to go through a period of probation to show whether I could submit to Party discipline. I attended the weekly meetings of the local Communist group. We met in a little room over a draper's shop in a back street of Fulham. Perhaps as a precaution against police inspection of the Party files or just to make it all more conspiratorial many comrades in those days used assumed names. Incredible though it now seems, I was known to the group of artisans, busmen, plumbers, shop assistants, building workers on building sites and a sprinkling of students from the London School of Economics as Comrade Fairy; Plute was given the name of Comrade Fish. The Secretary — a perky little woman, who invented these fancy names, must have had a sense of humour.

But they fitted us. Whereas I flew over the surface of Marxist ideology in which we were instructed by an earnest Jewish student, Comrade Fish plunged deep into the profundities of Surplus Value as though in his natural element.

The exhilaration of attachment to Lenin's Party, the Party to which Grisha had belonged, the spearhead of the militant working class, was tempered somewhat by being given the task of selling the *Daily Worker,* either at street corners, or in workers' tenements at the weekend. I am no saleswoman, as I'd shown long ago in a different way with the suffragette leaflets. I knew that the purpose of persuading people to buy a paper they didn't want was to increase sales of the *Worker* and gain new adherents to the Party, but that didn't make me like tramping up and down stone stairs, bumping into scampering children and being stared at by inquisitive or hostile eyes. I had to knock on doors without getting a response and have doors slammed impatiently in my face even before I could begin my set speech. So seldom did I sell a copy that rather than return with a batch of leftovers to the Secretary I took to shoving the paper, as though it were a circular, under the door or into a letter-box and paid myself out of my own pocket. No self-respecting Communist, I thought, would have stooped to such cowardice.

I returned late from my class at Woking one wintery evening to find the house in Oakley Street in darkness. After searching in vain in my handbag for the latchkey rather than wait on the doorstep for Plute's return from a Party meeting, I rang the other bells and receiving no answer tried again. I had given up hope when the door was suddenly flung open. A tall young man peered at me over the turned-up collar of a dressing gown. He enquired peevishly what I wanted. With my sweetest and most ingratiating smile I explained. 'I hope,' I added apologetically, 'I haven't got you out of bed.'

'You have,' he snapped irritably. 'I didn't expect to be disturbed at this hour. It's gone eleven.'

He slammed the door after me and as I followed him up the stairs I saw through the open door of his room shelves filled with books lining the wall. As though relenting, he paused a moment on the landing to warn me not to make a habit of losing my latchkey. Noticing a humorous twist of his lips, a twinkle in his eyes as he flicked back his hair, I promised to have a spare cut. I was about to climb up further to our flat when suddenly, to my astonishment, he invited me in to inspect his books.

The first thing I saw was a complete edition in separate volumes of Proust's *Remembrance of Things Past*.

'You have a marvellous collection,' I said enviously. 'How lucky you are to possess the whole of Proust.'

'Am I? Why?' Puckering his lips in a smile, he scratched his head nervously.

'Because I've longed to read him and never had a chance.' He hesitated a moment, and then taking down *Swann's Way* said I could borrow it.

I thanked him and suggested that to make sure he got it back he should call on us whenever he felt like it.

When he eventually did turn up the readiness with which he accepted Plute's invitation to stay to supper suggested he was either lonely or poor, or both. He was painfully nervous and shy. He came often after that. He seemed to find Plute's sturdy working-classness a relief. His public school accent was in striking contrast to Plute's. They shared a contempt for the middle classes, but Adrian from closer knowledge. He described his home environment as stifling.

His mother, who was an invalid in constant pain, idolized him as her only child. Now that he had left home to fend for himself as a freelance journalist, Adrian went home every second weekend, a penance for which he reckoned he deserved the small allowance he got from his father. Except for the rare holiday abroad he hadn't begun to live until he came to Oakley Street, nor had he met people with whom he felt so completely at ease as he did with us. When he learned I was living unmarried with Plute and had been ostracized for it by my parents he admired me as much as he did Plute. Plute thought him a namby-pamby mother's boy, but encouraged him partly because he was a possible convert for the party. In sharing an evening meal with us, he used to supply his own food. After a bit he became practically part of our household. I should have known better. But since Gibson had set up house with the girl he'd met at Curwens and Michael had left the school at Bristol for a more congenial Prep School at High Barnet near enough to London for either Gibson or myself to visit him regularly, I felt more relaxed about everything. I was happy to be the pivot on which our household turned.

Sending Michael to Bristol had been a bad mistake. He quite rightly blamed me for being so engrossed in my emotional life, before his father and I finally separated, that I went for a school recommended by a casual acquaintance. Both his father and I sacrificed him because we wouldn't take the trouble. I should have known from my own experience how wretched it can be for a child to be sent to the wrong school. He was persecuted by a bully of a master, a former army sergeant, who seemed to take pleasure in humiliating him. One incident in particular haunted him for years.

He had been given a small part in a play to be performed for parents and staff before the Christmas holidays. Anxious to do his best he'd made himself word perfect and was waiting in the wings during the dress rehearsal for his cue when one of the cast came bounding up behind him and pushed him headlong through part of the scenery. Whether it was on purpose or an accident he wasn't sure. The master in charge of the performance, without bothering to enquire who was to blame for damaging the scenery so soon before the night, flew at Michael. Not only did he give his part to someone else but to punish him still further made him a target for ridicule by placing him at the tail-end of the crocodile of boys that marched regularly through the centre of the city with his school blazer and cap worn inside out. It was torture. When we heard about it we immediately took steps to find an alternative school.

To try and make up for the humiliation he'd suffered at Bristol,

I gave him an entire new outfit for his new school. But his main grandeur he owed to himself. He became captain of the cricket team and as such he alone was entitled to an azure cap, with the initials of the school embossed in gold thread. At the end of the summer term parents were invited to attend a key match against a neighbouring school. Although I cared nothing for cricket I felt very proud when at the close of play he came racing across the field to the parents' enclosure, his azure cap at the back of his blonde head!

I was sitting shabbily dressed amongst wealthy and respectable middle-class parents. Michael was only there because of his Australian grandfather that I disliked so much. The Headmaster paid him a tribute as a thoroughly reliable wicket-keeper and then suggested his own previous career, the Navy, as a suitable one for Michael. He could then go on to Dartmouth. I assured him that as a pacifist I would never want my son to join the armed forces; but he was, of course, at liberty to choose for himself.

'It is premature yet,' he said, eyeing me with disapproval, 'to discuss the boy's future. But I am sure that whatever career he eventually chooses the qualities he shows as a wicket-keeper will enable him to make a success of it. You need have no fear for your son's future, Mrs Young.'

14 Crematorium

Adrian introduced Plute to Rabelais, and the two would chuckle over him like schoolboys. Accusing Adrian of being abnormally fussy about food, Plute christened him Picra — short for Picrahendipan — a nickname which suited him. At night, rather than go down two flights of stairs to the lavatory, I used to pee into a large earthenware jug. Plute had the idea of brewing tea from the contents of the jug, and passing it off on Adrian. He solemnly passed a cup to Adrian who took one sip and spat it out into his handkerchief.

'What's wrong?' Plute enquired innocently.

'The tea,' said Adrian, puckering up his face in disgust, 'it has a vile taste.'

'You shouldn't be so pernickety, Picra,' admonished Plute gravely. 'Drink it up.'

'I tell you it tastes like poison. Try it yourself.'

'An aphrodisiac like Edith's water tastes like poison? For shame, old chap.'

'You mean,' stuttered Adrian, flushing to the roots of his hair, as the truth dawned on him, 'that you've made the tea from her jug?'

'And why not, for God's sake? Urine is a perfectly innocuous liquid. If you don't believe me, ask a doctor.'

'I'll take Rabelais' advice,' said Adrian, smiling wryly. 'I'll boil down my keys and give you a dose of opening medicine. That should cure you of your dirty tricks.'

Our coat collars turned up against a wind that blew rain in our faces, we stood shivering amongst a crowd of mixed nationalities at the entrance of Golders Green crematorium waiting for the arrival of the body of Sakletvala, the veteran Parsee Communist Member of Parliament. Adrian had come with the intention of writing it up for a left-wing periodical. Plute to pay homage, myself from curiosity and because they had.

'A remarkable man, Sak,' said a venerable Parsee admirer behind us. 'A politician who used the parliamentary machine to further his own ends.'

'True. Very true,' squeaked his companion. 'Sak beat the British at their own game.'

Men bared their heads as the hearse bearing a coffin draped in a blood red flag over a purple pall surrounded by wreaths approached the gates. Behind the relatives' cars was a little procession of sympathizers with a Party banner, headed by Harry Pollitt. We didn't join the stampede to the chapel door so had to remain outside on the steps. A strong smell of incense and some weird, singsong chanting came from within.

'Why the hell all this mumbo-jumbo?' said Plute. 'Sak wouldn't have wanted it.' A slim girl in Punjabi trousers looked at him balefully. As the hypnotic rhythm of the Parsee singing sank slowly into silence, Pollitt began to speak. All we could catch were a few hackneyed phrases. We were turning away when someone in the crowd started the International. Standing to attention, Plute boomed out *Away with all your superstitions.* Adrian smiled ironically.

> Comrades come rally,
> The last fight let us face,
> The International unites the human race.

At this a sudden flood of emotion brought tears to my eyes. Everything seemed sad. Adrian looked at me anxiously. 'What's wrong, darling?' he whispered, clasping my hand for the first time.

Plute heard the concern in his voice and his endearment. 'Let's beat it,' he said with a scowl. He shoved through the loiterers at such a rate that he left us behind. He turned a deaf ear to us in the tube going home and on reaching the house dashed upstairs to our flat and slammed the door.

'What's upset him?' Adrian innocently enquired.

'Fed up about something I suppose.'

Advancing towards me as I entered our living room Plute gripped me by the shoulders and holding me taut against his chest enquired, 'What's going on between you and Picra?'

'Nothing.' I assured him, candidly returning his scrutiny. 'He is as attached to you as he is to me.'

'He doesn't hold *my* hand and call *me* darling.'

'Of course not. He's not a queer. He just thought I was upset at the funeral.'

'I'll take your word for it this time. But mind you,' he warned, releasing his grip, 'if I find your sensitive mother's boy making up to you on the quiet, he'll not be welcomed here. Understand?'

Aware that Plute's attitude had changed towards him after that incident at the funeral Adrian took himself off for a walking tour in the Chilterns. Only when he'd gone did I realize what an essential part of my life he'd become, primarily as a buffer between myself and Plute. In an effort to win me back wholly to himself he increased his sexual demands and when I was mechanical about it and therefore failed to satisfy him he would vent his resentment by attacking me. I was a cockteaser, a fraud. Worse — a succubus. I'd suck a fellow dry and when I'd had my fill chuck him aside as I would a bit of orange peel. My emancipation was another name for promiscuity. Rather than admit there was some truth in what he said I lashed out at him. We waged a wordy battle fought out to a finish in bed and in the act of love achieved a temporary peace.

One day my brother asked me to go and discuss an idea which had been simmering in his mind for months. He wanted premises suitable for his own gallery where he could exhibit his own work to a wider public than was possible at Wimbledon. Rents in the West End were too high. He suggested Chelsea instead. He wanted me, as I lived in Chelsea and had more time than Plute, to find a place with a shop front — preferably in the King's Road — with hanging space for twenty or more paintings. Though he and Flora would pay the rent to begin with, which shouldn't exceed five pounds a week at the most, Plute or any other artist whose work they jointly approved could also show there. Outsiders would pay a hanging fee and a percentage on sales. I was to try to get Gibson to persuade the art critic on the *Express* to give the opening show a write-up.

I'd almost given up in despair, but although I didn't pray this time I suddenly saw a 'To Let' board over the door of a green-grocer's shop in Bury Street where I used sometimes to buy vegetables. It had a fair sized bow-window, and behind the shop an adjoining room. Dilapidated though they both were I realized that if newly decorated it would do as a gallery. Plute's chief objection was the position. He didn't believe anyone, let alone a critic, would ever bother to come to a pokey little place in a back street of Chelsea. Ronald was agreeably surprised that the rent was only two quid a week. He thought we should give it a trial. 'Nothing venture, nothing win, old chap,' he said patting Plute vigorously on the back. I had a good idea. To attract people I suggested we should hold informal discussions on modern art, alternating with poetry readings to which we should invite regulars from The Poetry Book Shop in Bloomsbury. Plute approved. He doubtless thought he'd have an opportunity to air his political views.

The four of us set about the decorating. Buckets of whitewash and gallons of white paint transformed the dingy greengrocer's shop into a passing imitation of a gallery. Flora put down rush matting on the floors, a table and a couple of chairs. As there was already a sink with a tap in the back room, we had a gas-ring fitted for tea.

My Saturday afternoon pleasure was hunting for bargains in the Caledonian Market. You could buy for a few shillings something that would cost pounds now in the Portobello Road. I bought a silk evening dress for a shilling and a corduroy jacket that lasted me for years for half-a-crown. I saw a copper hurricane lamp on a stall and bought it for a couple of shillings, believing that it would do in the gallery at night. 'We're trying to sell pictures, not selling fishing tackle,' Plute reminded me sarcastically. But Flora was all for it and so was Ronald.

'Not at all a bad idea,' he said. 'It would be a symbol for the light of art we are striving to keep burning in an age of political conflict. We shall call the gallery The Hurricane Lamp.'

The lamp did its job. At night its flickering little flame drew the eye of passers by to a summer landscape by my brother flanked by a couple of Plute's charcoal sketches of nudes. It helped to get us a boost from a reporter on a local paper. He advised all those interested in art to step inside a delightful little gallery run by adventurous young artists under the sign of The Hurricane Lamp. Apart from acting as secretary Flora presided at the gallery on the days I was lecturing, and it was she who gave an interview to another reporter which appeared in the gossip column of the *Standard*. I don't know if that did it, but before a few months had passed the gallery was packed to overflowing for the Friday evening discussions on art and literature. My experience as a lecturer helped. The unpublished poems that I read, including a number by Adrian, I delivered with such intensity that even the mediocre, I thought, sounded impressive.

My brother was not content to run a debating society free of charge. Our first aim was to sell pictures; our second to make ourselves known to a wider public by starting a magazine. His enthusiasm carried the day. We produced a magazine which he as editor called *The Emotionist*. It summed up his belief that the intensity of emotional experience behind it, rather than the skill of it, should be the criterion of a work of art. From the material submitted by the members of our group he selected only those contributions which suited his theory. Apart from Plute, Adrian and myself there were the first-ever-published poems from the now famous Peggy Ashcroft and her brother, Edward. Plute designed the cover. We produced one copy. It is in the archives of the British Museum at Colindale as a never-seen memorial to The Hurricane Lamp.

I sat at a table in the gallery preparing a lecture. The door was pushed open to admit a prospective customer. I said 'Good afternoon', handed him a typed catalogue and as it was our rule never to pester anyone went on with my writing. I saw him out of the corner of my eye pick up a couple of Ronald's unframed canvases standing against the wall and examine them closely. The two he selected dated from Ronald's 'dynamic period'.

'These are interesting,' he said turning to me. 'Who's the artist?'

'R. O. Dunlop. The name's on the back.'

How could he get in touch with him? As luck would have it Ronald, who had been painting the Thames from the Embankment, came breezing in, his painting gear in a canvas bag slung from his shoulder, a smudge of paint on his cheek, a wet canvas in his hand. I introduced him to the man and upon my return from the back room where I had been making tea saw Ronald ushering him, the canvases he'd selected under his arm, into a waiting taxi. Almost falling over himself in jubilation he came back into the gallery and said,

'Who do you think that was?'

'A dealer?'

'Welenski, the art critic. He is taking my canvasses to the director of a Bond Street gallery. If, on the recommendation of a man as famous as Welenski, I'm given a show at the Redfern, as far as I'm concerned The Hurricane Lamp will have fulfilled its purpose. Once I've got started on a career in the art world I hope never to look back.'

We drank our tea to his success.

The Redfern did agree. The rest of us decided we could not keep on with the gallery. But before we finally shut up shop a particularly articulate member of the group persuaded me to organize a public meeting in the centre of London, at which a prominent member of the Communist Party would debate with a representative of the British Union of Fascists.

Plute refused to attend, let alone appear on the platform with a Fascist. The B.U.F. chose as their representative William Joyce who later became 'Lord Haw-Haw' in the second war. As Mosley's lieutenant he needed someone good against him and I could think of no-one more suitable than Humphrey Slater whom I'd heard speaking on dialectic materialism at Marx House. Slater was a Party organizer for Bermondsey and a man to be reckoned with intellectually. He habitually dressed like the lowest paid white-collar worker, or more precisely like an exaggerated likeness of Lenin— peaked cap, celluloid collar, wispy tie, nondescript jacket. With this went a film star profile, public school accent, a complexion of a pallor that was almost transparent and visionary blue eyes.

I'd heard he was a painter of talent who had given it up to devote himself to Party work and stood in awe of him. He was a Hero of our Time. When I met him at a café in the Grays Inn Road to discuss the proposed meeting I was to begin with literally tongue-tied. To break the silence I began asking irrelevant questions. Did he smoke? No. Did he mind if I did? Why should he? Did he choose to live in Bermondsey? Yes — with a Jewish family. As a painter did he mind living in ugly surroundings? His blue eyes glinted. It depended what I meant by ugly. He'd rather live in Bermondsey than Beverly Hills.

'Surely,' I persisted, 'the lack of an aesthetic sense in working class homes offends your eye?'

'Not in the least. I dropped the word aesthetic from my vocabulary when I gave up painting. By and large an aesthetic sensibility, taste — call it what you will — is a luxury the industrial working class has not yet had the means to cultivate. Taste depends on environment, on the class structure of society.'

Warned that he was about to lecture me I changed the subject to the meeting. He had such an air of bored resignation that I thought he must despise me as a middle class snob — until I mentioned Joyce. 'If it's Joyce they've chosen to defend their cause,' he said, 'I shall enjoy an opportunity of laying out that feather-brained heavyweight.'

The contest was in a room above a shoe store by Oxford Circus. It was the first time, within my knowledge, that an avowed Fascist and Communist had debated in public.

As Chairman I was seated on the platform, rigid with nervous tension. When Slater arrived people began to trickle in. The front rows of seats were occupied and the room more than half full and I had begun to suspect the B.U.F. had played a dirty trick on me and weren't coming when above the chatter in the room we heard the thud of booted feet stamping on the stairs. All heads turned to the door. Solemn as Grenadier Guards, a body-guard of Mosley's Blackshirts marched in single file into the room. Hooted at by the rest of the audience they lined up against the walls. I whispered to Slater: *'Their's not to reason why, their's but to do and die.'* He nodded in response and as I rose to introduce Joyce his bodyguard hailed him with the Fascist salute. With the slickness of a practised salesman he argued that the objective of Fascism was to substitute for the old, obsolete, ruling class a Corporate State, in which the interests of all classes should be represented not by a parliamentary system — which was for the most part a debating society — but by one party under the direction of a constitutionally elected leader.

'We don't want no Hitler here,' shouted a burly man at the back. Fascism, Joyce continued, unperturbed, would not legislate for one class of the community at the expense of another but would legislate for the nation as a whole. Unlike the communists, who advocated abolishing private property and nationalizing the means of production and distribution, Fascists believed that only by active co-operation and participation between workers and management in industry could socialism be achieved. A nation which respected social justice must maintain law and order, other-wise chaos would result. To prevent chaos, National Socialism could not tolerate a revolution based on the doctrines of the German Jew, Karl Marx and his followers, the Communists.

'The enemy in our midst,' he thundered, 'are the Jews. Cos-mopolitan Jewry has appropriated the wealth of every country in the world. Who runs Big Business? Who are the international bankers? The Jews.'

As murmurs of protest mingled with applause from the Black-shirts circulated through the room, saying that time was running short I hastily called on Slater to address the meeting. Quietly, with the dignified air of a professor addressing his students, he began by accusing Joyce of ignoring the class structure of capitalist society. Fascism he described as the outcome of monopoly capitalism in decline. The failure of an impoverished ruling class in the countries which had fought to form stable governments was responsible for the growth of Fascism in Europe. In psychological terms it was the result of an inferiority complex in a defeated nation, and in practical terms the result of the economic depression which followed the war. He blamed the Versailles Treaty for the breakdown of the German economy; that, and the threat of communism, had been responsible for the German ruling class selling out to Hitler — Hitler, whose anti-semitism, whose mock heroics and demagogy, Mosley's British Union of Fascists so fatuously imitated. Their tactics, and Hitler's, would bring Europe to another war.

Angry protests from Mosley's henchmen drowned the some-what feeble applause which greeted Slater. To avoid an open clash I immediately thanked the speakers, the audience for their friendliness, and declared the meeting closed.

My brother had reluctantly come with other of my supporters from The Hurricane Lamp. He waited for me with Adrian at the door. Adrian congratulated me on my handling of the meeting. Ronald thought it a waste of time. In his opinion there was nothing to choose between a Communist and a Fascist. They were opposite sides of the same coin.

I thought Plute's talent equal to that of Ronald. His failure was partly one of temperament. Ronald's faith in himself as a painter gave him a self-assurance which Plute, who doubted his, completely lacked. This would account for Plute renouncing his ambitions as a painter. When I said that I thought that funda-mentally he was an artist he said he'd rather be a plumber, a stonemason, anything other than a painter. All easel paintings would soon be replaced by applied art or murals. Colour photo-graphy had made ordinary painting out of date — hence the move towards abstract art, and that wasn't for him. I gave up trying to argue with him. The whole external world has always been a source of wonder to me. I turned to Adrian for sympathy.

In deference to Plute he had left Oakley Street for another furnished apartment in Chelsea. But I encouraged him to drop in at the Gallery on the days when it was my turn to look after it and took to meeting him for a stroll on the Embankment after closing hours. We were united by delight in the gulls or scenting the smell of the sea in the wind over the river. Adrian's lyrical temperament seemed to complement mine so perfectly that I could again be free to be myself. As water takes colour from the sky, so Adrian reflected each of my changing moods and I his.

Aware that I was rapidly assigning to him the role of second best, Plute retaliated by attacking me. I took shelter in silence as I had with Gibson. It didn't always work. We hate only those we love. The intensity of the hatred I had for Plute when he reduced me to tears equalled the intensity of the love I had felt for him in the beginning. He vented his fury on me by flinging me on the bed and keeping me pinioned beneath his weight until I yielded to a sort of rape. It was no use. It didn't give even him pleasure. After accusing me of sleeping with Adrian he once grasped me by the throat and looked so murderous that I thought he was going to strangle me. Rather than try escape, I closed my eyes in prayer. I prayed that he might be delivered from the fury that possessed him and that I might find a way of lessening his pain while leaving me free. I wanted it all ways.

'Praying to your God, are you, blast you?' he scoffed, laughing hysterically. 'Your hypocrisy sickens me. I've had my bellyful. You can go to your milksop, and good riddance.' He strode from the room and banged the door.

But Plute's shadow came between Adrian and me. When we met on the steps of the British Museum it was as though he stood in the portico to bar our way. That winter he'd taken to wearing a black overcoat to match his black artist's hat. He looked like a funeral. I wilted. The continual strain of our life together affected me physically. When no longer able to endure the menstrual pain I suffered, I consulted a gynaecologist recommended by Flora who diagnosed a prolapse of the uterus and advised an operation. Plute was against it. I was all for it. I welcomed a fortnight in hospital as a way of getting out of a situation that had become intolerable. My father (with whom I was on good terms again) offered to send me at his expense after the operation to a convalescent home run by a fellow Anthroposophist in the Tyrol. The *Kuranstalten,* ten miles from Innsbruck, was in a sunny valley ringed by snow-capped mountains. I had a room to myself. The window opened on to a balcony over flowery meadows and the golden cupola of the little whitewashed church of St Martin. A lime tree flanked the gate to its grassy precincts and it was under its scented shade that I rested before climbing uphill past the Stations of the Cross.

I returned after a month as suntanned as when I docked at Tilbury from Australia. I had expected Plute to meet me at Victoria, but there was no sign of him. Neither was he at the flat. The place was in chaos: a sink full of dirty crockery, the table stained with ink and littered with discarded layouts, ashtrays full of cigarette butts, pots of poster paint. The bed looked as if it had not been made for weeks. I had set about clearing up the mess when I heard the familiar tramp of hob-nailed boots. *Kinch, the knife blade* — which Adrian borrowed from Joyce's *Ulysses* to describe Plute when he was looking menacing — stood at the door. He kissed me perfunctorily, complimented me on looking like an advertisement for holidays abroad, and flinging his hat on the floor sank as though exhausted into an easy chair.

He had changed in my absence in some way, apart from having lost weight and looking so scruffy. He said that fending for himself was a bore but he expected he'd have to get used to it once he started to live on his own again. Puffing nervously at a cigarette, and avoiding my eye, he explained that he intended moving to a disused warehouse as far as I can remember near Chalk Farm. The brewer who owned the property and used the lower part as a storehouse had agreed to let the upper floor to him as a workshop for a nominal rent provided he had the roof repaired and did up the place.

'Whether I take it on or not,' he said, turning to me, 'depends on you. If you're still hankering after that effeminate mother's boy you're dying to seduce I won't stand in your way. I'm determined not to let you torment me as you have in the past. I've been a mug long enough.'

'Well,' he enquired, after a long silence, 'what's it to be? Picra or Plute?'

'Neither,' I replied in anger. 'I'll live by myself.'

'That's up to you.'

Our final leave-taking took place in his new 'studio'. To reach it we had to climb a staircase as steep as a ladder from the dark warehouse beneath. I couldn't help but admire him. Nobody else would have chosen that gloomy, ramshackle old barn of a place. Anchored against its walls were the oddments of heavy mahogany furniture he had borrowed from his aunt, a low divan on which a Paisley shawl made a splash of colour and in the window recess a draughtman's table. The only sign of domesticity was the gas-ring and griller he'd fixed up next to a sink over which he had hung a plate-rack and a few pots and pans.

'You don't think much of my hide-out?' he enquired.

'It's certainly uncompromising.'

'Good,' he said, rubbing his hands together in satisfaction. 'That suits me.'

I suggested with an attempt at levity that he'd very soon have a girl on his divan.

'Not any old bit of skirt, though,' he said gruffly. 'I'm looking for a girl with eyes like the sky, apple-blossom cheeks, sunny hair — a younger edition of you. But a sensible working class girl who won't think she's doing me a favour by taking me on.'

When as a member of the Communist Party he left London to join the art department of a Publishing Co-operative in Moscow, he passed out of my life as Grisha had done, and I was told he had married just such a girl as he'd described.

A precarious harmony marred by nervous tension caused in part by the difference in our ages pervaded the whole of the seven years Adrian and I lived together. So frequently did we change our flats that we became completely expert at it. Michael never knew where he'd be coming home to on his next holiday. One summer Adrian rented a coastguard cottage from Middleton Murry on the Dorset coast. We were happiest there. The mornings, and before supper in the evenings, we devoted to writing — I was trying to write as well as he; the afternoons to lazing on the shore or wading ankle deep through fields of buttercups to explore the countryside. By the time Michael came to stay with us on his way to his first term at Dartington School, Adrian had practically completed a book on the minor Elizabethan dramatists and I finished *Lisa*. Sustained by Adrian's never failing advice and encouragement I wrote that book with a speed and ease I have never since achieved. It was therefore fitting that I should take him as my hero.

The nearer I was to forty the more painfully was I aware of the lines, wrinkles, the sagging chin, thickening waist, protuberant belly. To compensate I became anxious to please, which never works. Yet, despite differences of age, common interests combined with respect for differences of personality which prevented us demanding more than either was willing to give helped us to get on well. When we finally settled down in a fine top flat in Guilford Street, Bloomsbury, I fondly imagined we might continue together indefinitely.

My parents who had thought Plute socially inferior were impressed by Adrian's middle class background, his public school accent, his shy and scholarly reserve. Adrian in the beginning suggested I should urge Gibson for a divorce so that he could marry me. His parents might then accept me. His mother called me the tart. But Adrian didn't press it and when eventually my father, wanting in his declining years to see me settled, offered to pay for a divorce his love had already begun to wane. I had learned to accept his almost neurotic obsession with food, his petulance if a meal was late, the nervous irritability which he ascribed to fatigue, as the price I had to pay for living with a writer. It wasn't until he became increasingly aloof that I began to suspect he was hiding something from me. One evening on returning from a lecture and finding him busy at the gas-stove preparing supper I went to have a wash in the bathroom. On lighting the geyser I knocked a matchbox off a shelf and as I stooped to pick it up saw a powder puff and lipstick lying on the floor. I stood staring at them in my hand for so long that Adrian called out irritably that my supper was getting cold. Before I had recovered he appeared at the door.

'What is keeping you in here? Didn't you hear me call?' he cried in exasperation. Then as soon as he became aware of my expression, he changed his tone to one of concern. What was the matter? Was I feeling unwell?

'You've been deceiving me, Adrian,' I said gravely. Holding out the tell-tale objects displayed in my hand I told him to return them to whoever they belonged to.

'Oh,' he said flushing, and wrinkling up his brow in disgust, 'that silly girl has left her cosmetics behind, has she?'

Snatching the powder puff from me and flinging it on the floor he wrapped me in his arms. I mustn't take his affair with Suzanna seriously.

'Who is she?' I demanded. An artists' model whom Plute had introduced him to in The Hurricane Lamp days. He had met her again at the Blue Cockatoo Cafe on the Chelsea Embankment and over coffee had tentatively suggested that she should call at the flat. To his surprise the very next week she had turned up on the doorstep. Naturally he'd invited her in.

'And she turned up again?'

He nodded.

'So naturally you made love to her?'

'That's what she came for. What else could I do?'

His self-satisfaction stung me afresh.

Pressing his cheek to my hair and kissing my forehead he pleaded to be forgiven. He couldn't bear to see me upset.

'Are you in love with the girl?' I asked fiercely, tugging his hair.

'Certainly not. She's a voluptuous little thing — all curves and dimples, like one of Renoir's nudes. Sexually attractive, otherwise dumb. You've nothing to worry about, so forget it and come and rescue the supper I have taken such pains to prepare.'

How could I forget it? I knew it was the beginning of the end. Every time he went out on his own I imagined he had a date with the girl. I didn't dare make love to him in case he should find me sexually inferior to her. Since this body, I thought, running a hand over my sagging breast, no longer gives him pleasure, it's time I left. But it's not easy to disentangle two lives which had been so closely entwined as ours had over the years. I had a dose of the medicine I had given to others in the past. It was slow-working and painful.

I'd taken on one thing from my father — a belief in the law of *Karma* — in the sense of *as ye sow that also shall ye reap.* It operates as surely as the law of gravity. But it did not make me accept any more philosophically Adrian's disclosure that he'd fallen in love with a girl whom he hoped eventually to marry. Turning his back on me, he began knocking out his pipe on the grate. Reflected in the mirror above the mantelpiece, I caught a glimpse of my face. It looked ghastly. His eyes too that met mine in the glass were those of a stricken deer. He was suffering as much as I. I knew it was useless to make a scene. He couldn't, he said penitently, help it. It just happened. He'd met her at a concert at the Queens Hall; they started talking in the interval, and he felt he just couldn't let her go without arranging to see her again.

'Love at first sight,' I remarked drily. 'I know. I've experienced it myself.'

'It was, I suppose,' he confessed. 'She's beautiful — in a way — like Michelangelo's Sybil. Tall, fair, and bursting with vitality. I didn't want to hurt you by telling you till I was sure of myself and her.'

'Have you fixed a date for the wedding day?'

'Oh, darling, of course not. There's no hurry. Stella is prepared to wait. She's tied up herself with a young Jewish artist. Because she believes he has talent, which I don't, she has been supporting him on an allowance from her family and from lecturing, as you do, at evening classes. Her subject is the History of Art. With a Cambridge degree she is quite capable of earning a living that will make her independent of me.'

'A wife without responsibility! What could be more convenient? The only snag is that she'll have to get rid of her protégé before you can take her on. At least that will give me a breathing space in which to find alternative accommodation.' I spoke bitterly.

He slunk from the room. I stared out of the window. Arc lamps in the street threw streaks of amber on the houses opposite leaving those in a side street dark as slabs of basalt. It stood for the fragility of all human relationships. Choking back a sob, I turned to the firelight that played upon shelves with Adrian's books on them, to his armchair, to the table we had bought together at an auction, to the hearthrug I had purchased for a few shillings in the Caledonian market. Each object told its own tale of an hour, a day or a year of the life we had spent together.

My mother's death shocked me out of my self-pity. Less than a week before I'd received a telegram from my father summoning me to the hospital where she lay dangerously ill of a brain haemorrhage, I had called to see her at the house in Cheyne Row, Chelsea, to which my parents had moved from Tite Street. Recovering from an attack of 'flu, she was sitting up in bed, enjoying tea, buttered toast and a boiled egg. She told me to fetch a cup and join her. There was plenty of tea left in the pot. 'There is nothing,' she said, 'I enjoy more than a really new-laid egg.'

After I had removed the tray and propped her up on the pillows, she said that during her trip to the Tyrol in the summer she had learnt something new about herself. She saw clearly that unless she gave love to others, she couldn't expect to receive love; that, on the whole, she had been a hard, selfish woman, and mean into the bargain. She had never regarded father's money as her own, and as he gave it away so lavishly to the Anthroposophical Society she thought it her duty to save as much as she could from household expenses. I couldn't understand what was behind it. It was out of character. It disturbed me more than the old harshness.

'Many's the hard word I've said to you,' she confessed. 'Can you forgive me?'

I told her I'd given back as good as I got. The trouble with us was that we were too much alike.

'True enough,' she admitted. 'I expect I envied you the courage to do the things I would have liked to do but did not dare. At least you've lived fully, and that's more than I can say of myself. Are you happy with Adrian?'

'Kiss me,' she entreated as I was turning away to hide my embarrassment, 'and let's be friends.' The texture of the cheek to which I pressed my lips had the softness of my grandmother's. 'It's odd,' she whispered, smiling and tugging nervously at my coat collar, 'that just as I'm nearing the grave father's love has given me a new lease of life. He has not made love to me for years as he did last week. It was wonderful — just like old times.'

'Oh mother,' I cried, hugging her, 'I'm so glad . . . .'

The tick of the wall clock in the cheerless hospital room emphasized the silence. A sister in blue ushered in my father. He had returned from mother's bedside. He warned me that mother was in a coma and would not last long. I followed the sister to a lift and through a long disinfectant-smelling corridor to a room off a ward. Promising to return shortly, she placed a chair for me by the bed. Light from a shaded lamp on the wall behind fell on mother's silvery silken hair, on an exposed width of brow. A lifelike tinge of rose on her cheeks didn't go with the shuddering gasps from her open mouth. She heaved in her effort to expel her breath from lungs that wheezed like a bellows. Her hand lay on the sheet like a withered leaf. Choked by tears, I pressed it to my cheek and there was a rattling whistle from dilated nostrils. The very air about us seemed to rock with her effort to breathe.

'God breathed into man the breath of life' say the scriptures. Man's breath is, and is no more. I clung to her from whom I had come into the world.

15 Bloomsbury

Mother's death detached me finally from Adrian and lessened the pain of leaving him. My father offered me a room to myself at the house in Cheyne Row. It was a large, comfortably furnished room under the eaves. I looked out on a pub. From the open window I could smell autumn in the air and catch a glimpse of the Thames. If it had been loneliness that had prompted father to invite me to the house he didn't show it. Though he had aged and complained more than before of stomach trouble which he said was an ulcer, he became ever more deeply involved in anthroposophical activities. I scarcely saw him except at breakfast on Sunday. Faithful little Elsie was still there as his housekeeper. She felt a kind of unacknowledged wife; and in proportion as he faded, she blossomed. She didn't like me being there. I might well have gone into the sort of depression of a discarded woman approaching middle age if what my mother had called my 'happy disposition' had not saved me.

The Communist Party had become more of a mass party and was trying to form a united front against Fascism. I had no difficulty in being enrolled as a member. With a Party card as a passport I crossed a frontier into a public life. I became, as I thought, committed. I was invited by the librarian at Marx House to attend a school at a country mansion in the heart of Somerset, and jumped at it.

Patricia Mills — a woman of about my own age and the only one with whom I felt a kinship amongst my new acquaintances in the Party — took me in her car. Apart from being half Irish like myself and sharing a disrespect for authority, Patricia was my opposite. She kept a tight hold on her emotions lest they betray her. I gave mine free rein. I was hesitant in attacking a political opponent. She went for him full tilt. She was reticent about her marriage to a wealthy business man. But I suspected that dissatisfaction with her married life had driven her into the Party; that, childless, she had adopted the comrades as her family.

To be with Patricia was like being out on a fine morning. We set out in her little Morris to race through summer country to our destination and arrived just in time for a noisy, slap-dash, communal tea in a huge dining room, its grandeur successfully dismantled for the occasion. I found myself seated next to a Russian girl. How she came to be present I do not know. Stolid, plain, with a snub nose and mousey hair scraped back from a low forehead she spoke excellent English with a guttural accent. As she was the only Russian I had met since Grisha I gushed over her. Absorbed in loading her bread with plum jam she paid no attention to my naïve remarks about her wonderful country. Then suddenly she startled me.

'In Russia,' she said, 'a private person is considered an idiot.'

'Idiot!' I exclaimed with a dry puff of laughter. 'Why idiot?'

'For the simple reason that a person who believes his private life is more important that the life of the community is an idiot.'

'Do you think the cap fits?' I asked fearfully. How awful if she thought me a private person.

I had been apprehensive of meeting such a well-known Marxist as Page Arnot: but when he came trotting up like a ballet dancer to greet Patricia and myself my fears vanished. He enlisted us into sweeping out the dormitories which last week's people had left disgusting, the floors littered with cigarette butts, fluff, wisps of paper, hairpins and even soiled sanitary towels under the beds. This was the life of the community.

We saw his sleeping accommodation. Amazed that it consisted of a camp bed in the corner of a small airless attic I protested vehemently. It was insulting to give the Director of Studies such a room. He should not put up with it. He chuckled, and laying a hand on my shoulder said he saw no reason why a lecturer should be treated as though he were superior to his students. I don't know whether it was he who appointed François Lafitte, the natural son of Havelock Ellis, as my instructor in dialectical materialism. François was as impatient as I was to be quit of the classroom and out in the sun. He passed me on to an elderly bricklayer. His nails encrusted with the grime of his calling, skin as wrinkled as a walnut, hair that looked as though powdered with lime, he tried patiently to hammer into my thick head Marx's theory of Surplus Value. If I came away from that summer school with but a dim idea of Marxist economics at least I had the privilege of seeing how a classless society could work.

For the happy years Michael spent at Dartington he is indebted as much to Gibson's sister, Florence, and the favourite daughter I mentioned before, as he is to his Australian grandfather. She was the wife of a clergyman who had been appointed Head of Achimota College in Accra. She was very interested in modern education. On a tour of inspection of English schools she had been to see Dartington and had given such an enthusiastic report of it that both Gibson and his father had been persuaded that Michael would be less likely to suffer from the consequences of a broken marriage at Dartington than at a more conventional school.

He had sprung from a gawky schoolboy into a tall, lanky youth with the sadness of adolescence in his eyes. I was hard pressed to keep him in clothes or to keep pace with his mind. Despite the affection we had for one another communication between us wasn't easy. I knew as little about his emotional life as he of mine.

Dartington opened a new life to him in which I had little part. He was growing rapidly closer to Dorothy Elmhirst (to whom, together with her husband, the school owed its existence) than he was to me; her family was becoming his family; she, as his good, bountiful mother, had taken the place of his own wayward, erring mother. I tried not to resent it.

After Michael had left Dartington to take up law I left my father's house for a flat in Great James Street in Bloomsbury so that I could provide him with a home.

A stink of tomcats and garbage cans in backyards hit you in the face as soon as you entered the oak panelled hall to climb to our two rooms. Their well-proportioned windows looked out on the grime of brick and waste pipes of surrounding houses. The cream panelling of the walls, the sloping floor and deep window embrasures, gave to the rooms the charm of a more gracious age. Michael could not understand what had decided him to take up law as a profession.

'I don't suppose,' he said, smiling quizzically and scratching his brow, 'I shall practise as a barrister. A law degree is simply a means to an end; useful for a political career, or for any other profession I may choose later in life.'

'You're determined to succeed.'

'I am if I can,' he confessed. 'I've seen enough of you and Gibson to know that your bohemian way of life is not for me. I'm ambitious. I want to leave my mark on life.'

'Good for you! I'm all for it providing your health can stand the strain.'

'You don't really approve, do you?' he questioned. 'You're disappointed? You'd prefer me to be an artist?'

'I believe in you implicitly, Michael. It's natural that you should react against your parents. I have enough faith in you to know that whatever you do, you will do well.'

Gibson had been so plagued by asthma in recent years that in desperation he was driven to take his doctor's advice and return to Australia. Things hadn't been going well with his girl.

'I'll either be cured by the sun or killed by boredom,' he confessed with melancholy resignation when he called at Great James Street after a farewell luncheon with Michael at the Inns of Court. 'It's bad enough to leave London, but to be separated from Michael is hell. He has promised that if I don't return in a couple of years, he'll take a trip to Australia.'

'He will,' I assured him.

'Look after him,' he said huskily, 'He's all I have left in the world.'

A pain, sharp as the exposed nerve in a tooth, tugged at my heart. I avoided looking at him.

'Has it ever occurred to you . . .' he hesitated, bit his lip, took a deep breath and gasped, 'that we might come together again some day.'

'You never know. It's possible,' I said brightly, evasively. A stranger's lips brushed mine. He turned and I watched him, holding his breast, slowly descend the dark staircase. As soon as he could no longer hear me I wanted to call him back. I wanted to comfort him, to promise to go to him should he send for me. I also knew it was too late; too late to blow on a love that had died a natural death. I suppose if I could have foreseen that within a year he would die I would have done more. He died of heart failure in a Melbourne hospital during a severe attack of pneumonia and just after he'd got one of the best jobs he'd had — Musical Director of the Australian Broadcasting Commission. On the night before a cable came from his father telling me about his death I woke in the early hours, sat up in bed, and was startled to see a shadowy figure, the head and shoulders distinctly etched against the oak panelling of the bedroom door. Thinking that perhaps Michael had returned late from a party and had looked in to see whether I was awake I called out to him. 'Is that you, Michael?' As there was no answer I got up, switched on the light and crossed the landing to his room, only to find him fast asleep in bed. No one else was around. It occurred to me afterwards that should there be survival after death, what more likely than that Gibson's spirit should visit those he loved most? For months afterwards the knowledge that he had died amongst strangers in a hospital ward filled me with remorse.

His father's death had a curious effect on Michael. He couldn't make himself speak of him for over a year. He seemed to be suffering from delayed shock.

It was through Adrian that I met Mulk Raj Anand, the Indian novelist and art critic, a volatile little man regarded in the thirties as a spokesman in Britain for the depressed millions of his countrymen in India. Many an evening in all seasons we met at closing time in the portico of the British Museum. His face seemed to express his soul. He talked so incessantly that it was difficult to get a word in, about his boyhood in Amritsar and the humiliations he had suffered from landladies when he first arrived in Cambridge. He was determined to describe the evils of a caste system which he said (unlike Mr Emerson) was worse than our class system in a novel he was writing when we first met him, called *Untouchable*. He read out portions of it to us after a curry in his room over a second-hand bookshop in a cul-de-sac off Southampton Row. Though his perpetual effervescence often wearied Adrian, he was flattered to have the finished manuscript submitted to him for criticism before it was offered to a publisher. 'I was taught Lord Macaulay's English at college in India and I find myself writing in his style,' he confessed with one of his winning smiles. 'I appeal to you to cure me of a bad habit. Correct my English. I give you carte-blanche.'

Adrian was hard-pressed to get through the pile of manuscripts he was reading for a publisher and asked me to do it. I tried to put it in more colloquial English and as a reward Mulk dedicated his *Untouchable* to me.

Social realism was the vogue in the thirties. Quick to cash in on it, Mulk followed the publication of *Untouchable* with his picaresque novel, *The Coolie*.

His account of the hardships, misery and degradation suffered by the masses of India was a great success.

In his room I met members of the Indian Progressive Writers Group, Ellen Wilkinson, the Labour MP for Jarrow, and Krishna Menon, then a Labour Councillor for St Pancras. One of the most articulate was a man called Iqbal Singh who was introduced to me by Mulk as a namesake of the Muslim poet, Mohammed Iqbal.

His black hair, his glowing eyes, the set of his head like that of a young bull about to charge made such an immediate appeal to my romantic notion of what a young poet should be that I hadn't eyes for anyone save him. He had left Cambridge in disgust at racial and class prejudice to care for himself in London and work as a freelance journalist. His knowledge of English and European literature made it difficult to realize that he was the son of an orthodox Sikh who had been the Governor of a penal settlement in the Andaman Islands.

He trusted me — I was more Irish than English. Otherwise he would never have fondled my hair, slipped an arm round my waist in public, and above all, showed me the MS of a story he intended to submit for publication to the Indian Progressive Writers Association. The story — *When one is in it* — with a frontispiece designed by his friend Roland Penrose appeared in a limited edition. Written in the genre required by the L.P.W.A. the action takes place in the annexe of a Bombay cotton mill during the monsoon. Amongst the workless hundreds applying to be taken on as loom hands is a young pregnant woman. Iqbal's insight into her mind astonished me. It revealed a new side of his nature for me. I feel pretty sure that if he'd not been driven by financial necessity to become a journalist he would have produced the most powerful novel yet to come from India. In his book on Buddha (which he dedicated to me) he discusses the teaching of Gautama — the man — against the social and historical background of the period; Buddhism as a reform movement within the context of a corrupt Brahmanism, rather than as a new religion.

Iqbal altered my life, and I his, in ways we didn't expect. I invited him to spend a couple of weeks with me at a cottage at Mousehole in Cornwall which I had rented from a friend for the summer. During his visit Patricia and her husband came for a weekend to a guest-house in the village and as I was expecting

them for supper, I sent Iqbal down to the pub to fetch a couple
of pints of beer. He was gone so long that I wondered what had
happened. Leaving the mackerel I had grilled to keep warm in
the oven I went to the gate to look for him. The sun had set.
Fishing smacks were making for the harbour mouth. Iqbal was
padding up the hill like a lion of the Punjab Pat and husband
following. Even as I scolded them for spoiling the supper I
guessed right away by the sparkle in Pat's eyes and Iqbal's that
they had not only met and been drinking in the bar but had fallen
in love. I could tell by the odd smile like that of children who
shared a secret.

When on my return to London Iqbal called to see me I came
straight to the point. 'You're in love', I challenged. 'Come now,
own up. You're in love with Pat.'

He didn't deny it. He ruffled my hair and grinned from ear
to ear.

'And is she in love with you?' I asked 'What's going to happen?
Does she intend leaving her husband?'

Nothing was settled, but they were planning to go to India
together next year. He wanted Pat to see the country and meet
his family.

Struggling to master my envy of Pat, I gave him my blessing.

I was hurrying down Charlotte Street on a murky November
evening when I saw Iqbal crossing the road to greet me. He was
on his way to meet a friend for supper in an Italian restaurant in
Soho. Would I join him?

'Do,' he entreated. 'You will like my friend Raja. I am sure
you will find you have much in common. We were at college
together at Lahore, but after I left India for Cambridge and he
for the Sorbonne, we lost touch with each other. This is our first
reunion.'

Taking my arm he marched me towards Soho, towards Raja,
towards India. In the crowded restaurant a slight man wearing a
black *sherwani* buttoned neatly to his chin, hair as luxuriant as a
girl's reaching to his shoulder, his eyes downcast, as though deep
in contemplation, was waiting. Iqbal's genial, 'Hello Raja, I've
brought an Irish friend to meet you,' called forth a smile that
transformed him.

I discovered at supper that apart from nationality and the fact
that they were both strict vegetarians the sole bond that united

Iqbal and Raja was the memory of their student days. Raja bore no grudge against the British. He admired London which, for so long, had been the home of refugees of all nationalities. He thought the squares, so unexpected in their setting of drab houses, delightful. He knew no city in the world so rich in green.

Iqbal was more interested in colour prejudice than colour. He said he knew of no European city where the colour prejudice was so noticeable.

'You should congratulate yourself,' he said truculently, 'on having chosen France as your adopted country.'

'And a French woman for wife?' suggested Raja playfully. 'I understand you intend to live with an English girl.'

'Irish,' corrected Iqbal. 'We share the ignominy of belonging to a subject race. Like Edith, Pat is a born rebel.'

'My Brahmanic soul greets the ancient Celt I see in Edith's eyes,' said Raja, raising a glass of lemonade to his lips. 'We belong to the same root race. Originally we were Aryans.'

On hearing that I had learnt about Hindu philosophy from my parents in my youth, he dismissed theosophy as journalism. But he said it had prepared me for India — for a ride in a bullock waggon through the jungle to his village, I laughed incredulously.

'I mean it,' he said, fixing me with embarrassing intensity. 'When I allow myself to trust my intuition it usually proves to be right.'

'Village women,' he continued in a hypnotic, nasal singsong, 'will be going at "cow dust hour" to fill their pitchers from the well; cattle driven from the fields by a young herdsman will raise the dust to a cloud of gold. A Brahmin expounds the wisdom of the Vedas to the village headman; an old priest, squatting on the stupa of a temple to Siva, offers his bowl for alms. Old women sieve grain at doorsteps. My grandmother, if she's still in the land of the living, will salaam to Edith as reverently as if she is a goddess in disguise; and my sweet sister, stooping over the hearth preparing the evening meal, will shake back her dusky hair to greet us with one of her most radiant smiles. Under the moon, which makes day of night, we crouch at the knee of that old grandmother of mine to hear her tales of gods and demons.'

'Shall we make my fairy tale come true?' he asked, smiling and pinching the tip of a wide nostril between finger and thumb of his wedding-ring hand.

'You talk,' I said, glowing with enthusiasm, 'like a poet. Do you write poetry?'

All prose of value, he replied sententiously, is like poetry. He himself wrote as nearly as possible to the rhythm of speech. He had written his novel *Kanthapura* in his native Kanarese and then translated it into English. His wife was now working on a French translation.

'How's it going?' Iqbal politely enquired. 'The fact that E. M. Forster acclaimed it so warmly should send up the sales a bit.'

Raja remarked with assumed humility that Forster had been most kind; but if he did not grow rich on the royalties he had come to collect from the publisher, to have seen Iqbal again and in particular to have met Edith had made his trip to London more than worthwhile.

He came to see me frequently during the following weeks. His visits were like seances. He initiated me into an esoteric world where even the most trivial incident had special significance. His vitality awakened my imagination. I took wing and soared — to be let down after one of the most miserable years of my life at his invitation on the station at Menton in the South of France.

When Michael had been hampered in his studies by the number of my friends always calling at the flat, in self-preservation he too decided to leave and went first to Toynbee Hall in the East End, and later to share digs with a friend from L.S.E. where Michael had now gone. Without his grant, the rent of the flat at Great James Street was beyond me. I caged myself in an ugly small room in a lodging-house near Kings Cross. Never had I been so depressed. The menopause added to my bleakness of spirit. Despite my belief in Communism as an ideal I had become increasingly critical of Party tactics. To say the end justified the means was to my mind Jesuitical. As I was a humanist before I was a communist, I felt I couldn't stomach it. All this was prompted by the trials in Russia of the veteran Bolsheviks who, under Lenin, had been the originators of the Revolution. I was afraid to say what I felt lest I should lose even my new friends. But I ceased to attend weekly meetings and let my contributions to Party funds lapse. I was naturally written off, considered a sentimental idealist, a romantic revolutionary.

Iqbal's and Pat's departure for India, combined with my father's death, increased my isolation.

When summoned by Ronald to the private Nursing Home

where my father lay dying of acute peritonitis I stood by the door, paralysed by awe. It took time to realize that the mask-like countenance, crowned by the wild hair of a prophet spread out on the pillows, was that of my father. His hands were crossed, his eyes closed as though deep in meditation, his lips drawn in a harsh line. Such '*a terrible beauty was born*' that I could not connect it with death.

As I tiptoed up to the bed he slowly, reluctantly opened his eyes. I clasped his hand and noticed the tattoo-mark from Glasgow, and as I held it in mind a faint flicker of recognition appeared in the depths of his eyes.

Eyes that had twinkled at me through pince-nez, eyes that had watched me quizzically, or gravely, eyes far off and blue of the boy who had run barefoot on the shores of Arran — eyes beyond the grave returned my gaze. I couldn't bear it. With a swift movement of recoil I backed away from the bed and stumbled from the room.

Sorrow turned Elsie's head. When my brother and I called in a taxi at Cheyne Row to take her to the Crematorium we found her in a state of euphoria, clad in widow's weeds, a beatific smile on her lips, a perfect red rose-bud pinned to her withered breast.

She was acting the part of a bereaved wife, writing the prelude to her own tragic end. Father had died intestate; and when the house at Cheyne Row with its furniture and effects had been disposed of and the riverside bungalow at Bray sold to pay off his debts Elsie took a job as nursemaid to a young married couple with a baby. Grief at being turned out of father's house must have shattered what reason was left in her poor fuddled head. It was from an evening paper I learnt to my horror that the police had been searching for a nursemaid — giving Elsie's address — who had disappeared with a baby while its parents were away for a weekend. Following the clue of an empty pram hidden amongst bushes on Wimbledon Common not far from the White Lodge, they had dragged the pond. In the slime and weeds at the bottom they had found the drowned bodies of Elsie and the child.

My sister, in mourning becoming to her delicate complexion and fair hair, waited with me in the dismantled house in Cheyne Row for the arrival of a van to collect for storage the oddments of furniture we had managed to salvage from the sale.

The empty rooms resounded as loudly with our memories as with our footfalls. Neither of us had any regret in quitting a house we had never really liked. We discussed our future. My sister expected to go to Cambridge to join friends who had recently started a restaurant. I had rented a bedsitter commanding a view of a square which, like myself, had seen better days, in a sleazy apartment house near King's Cross. The last people I would have expected to rescue me were my father's employers. A solicitor's letter informed me that it had been unanimously decided to purchase a life annuity for me and my sister in acknowledgment of my father's years of service to them,

Our fortune wasn't as good as it seemed. My sister had three pounds a week, and myself one pound. When my first quarterly instalment swelled my dwindling bank account, I moved to a flat at the top of a house in Charlotte Street. I took the flat because of a window in the back room. It jutted over roof tops to a wide wash of sky that made me feel I was on board ship. Raja took his leave of me, at that window, on the eve of his departure to India. 'This is not goodbye, Edith,' he assured me. 'Just as I believe we have met and known each other in our past lives on earth, so I believe we shall meet again in this incarnation.' He promised that when the time was ripe for me to come to India, he would send me word.